Learn to Belly Dance Textbook & Certification Program

Learn to Belly Dance Textbook & Certification Program

Dance Lessons & Choreographies for Students, Troupes, Performers & Dance Instructors

Shalimar Ali

To order additional copies of this book, contact:
Xlibris Corporation
1-888-795-4274
www.Xlibris.com
Orders@Xlibris.com
95428

Contents

DEDICATION

This book is dedicated to my family for their support, encouragement and participation in dance with me throughout the years. They made my dream of dancing come through. A special thanks to Lena, Adolph, Gina and Vance, Forestine and Uncle George (Nookie), who are smiling from Heaven. Also thanks to Pam, Reggie, Ben, Candy, Chonnie, Brenda, Ernestine, Chell, Tina, Lena, Tai, Tia, Toya, Alicia, Deja, Danielle & Tyrese and every family member that danced, drummed, dreamed and supported this journey in my life. A Special thanks to Cheryl Kellett, my former student who did the lovely drawings for this book. This book would not be possible without all of the dancers that I have taught, all of the dancers I have studied from and all of the dancers from across the world who share a special interest in Belly Dance!

Chapter 1

Introduction

Brings up the question: *Why did I write this book?* After several years of Middle Eastern dance training, I began teaching classes at a local community center. It took me several years to improve and perfect my teaching skills. Remembering my days as a "beginning dance student" helped tremendously. Back then, it was so difficult to remember each new step learned, or match-up movements with their appropriate names. Writing notes in class was one thing—if you had the time to write notes. Wouldn't it be so easy if you already had the notes written for you—then in class you could concentrate on the movements taught, later when you practiced at home-you could use the notes to review what was taught in class. Of course, a book could never replace a "live" teacher or class-you wouldn't have corrections, competition, or encouragement. So, here's hoping that this "collection" of notes would give you-the student exactly that-more time to dance in classes and pre-written notes for your practice sessions at home.

When I was a beginning student, something that really helped me out was a book I'd brought entitled *"The Compleat Belly Dancer"* (by Julie Ruskin and Marta Schill). In my opinion, it did for belly dancers what Webster had done for a lot of others: help standardize our belly dance "language." And speaking of Webster, his definition of dance is: "to move". DANCING means many things to many different people. To me, dancing is a form of self-expression, utilizing various parts of your body to execute various movements. Dancing can be performed "intrinsically" (for self), or "publicly" (for the pleasure of others); and can take many forms or fashions, depending on its origins (ballet, break dance, tap, jazz, Tahitian, Spanish, Middle Eastern, Ballroom, modern, square dance, Hawaiian, Indian, etc.); but what makes it great is the individuality of each performer.

What Is/Why Belly Dance?

What is Belly Dance? The dance which Americans know as "belly dance" has gone by many names. The French who found the dance named it "dance du ventre" or dance of the stomach. It is known in Greece as the cifte telli (also the name of a Turkish rhythm), in Turkey as "rakkase" and in Egypt as "Raks Sharqi." Middle Easterners also call it "danse orientale" to distinguish it from the "balady" or country dance. After its appearance at the Chicago Exposition at the turn of the century, Americans discovered it and the French name, danse du ventre, was translated into the "Belly Dance." [Excerpted from *"The World's Oldest Dance"* by Karol Henderson Harding.]

Today, Belly Dance is a fun way to exercise and shimmy pounds away. Men and Women of all sizes, ages and backgrounds take Belly Dance classes for fun, exercise or profit. In America and across the world, thousands of Middle Eastern Dance performers entertain audiences at Greek & Arab restaurants, Festivals, Fairs and other Theatrical productions. Add something new to your exercise menu, and learn about new cultures at the same time.

I like to think of Belly Dance as a smorgasbord of dances from many different countries. A dance student can learn many different dance styles, that all fall under the category of Belly Dance. The dance music and styles can come from Greece, Morocco, Egypt, Turkey, Africa, Lebanon, etc. American dancers, in fact, have re-invented Belly Dance by adding unique and individual touches to the dances from those countries. Let's take a magic carpet ride and explore Belly Dance!

Dance Technique Checklist

Please fill this out before you start training to keep track

Student Name: _____

Training Began? (Month _____, Year _____); Instructor: _____

Goals (check all that apply):

Solo Performer ____, Group Performer ____ Instructor ____

#	Description	Notes or Choreography Used In	Completed?	Date Completed
1.)	Before Dance Warm-Up			
	a.) Pushme/Pullme			
	b.) Upper Body Twist Stretch			
	c.) Six-Way Body Stretch			
	d.) Floor Stretch			
2.)	DANCE MOVEMENTS			
	a.) Head/Neck			
	b.) Arms/Shoulders			
	c.) Rib Cage/Torso			
	d.) Hips			
	e.) Floorwork			
	f.) Footwork/Turns			
3.)	DANCE MOVEMENT VARIATIONS			
	a.) Add bounce			
	b.) Add hop			
	c.) Add shimmy			
	d.) Add thrust			
	e.) Add undulation			
	f.) Add vibration			
	g.) Angle of movement			
	h.) Combine movements			
	i.) In place or travel			
4.)	DANCE MOVEMENT TRANSITIONS			
	a.) Angle change			
	b.) In place or travel			

	c.) Level change			
	d.) One movement into another			
	e.) Smooth vs. Sharp transitions			
5.)	FLOOR PATTERNS			
	a.) Type of Stage/Venue			
	b.) Square pattern			
	c.) Circular pattern			
	d.) Spiral pattern			
	e.) Front to back			
	f.) Side to side			
	g.) In place or travel			
6.	PROPS/SPECIALTY			
	a.) Veil Dancing			
	1. Types of (straight, circular, split, cape)			
	2. Fabric considerations			
	3. Drapes			
	4. Veil Movements			
	5. Discard			
	b.) Cane Dancing			
	c.) Sword Dancing			
	d.) Candle Dancing			
	e.) Other, misc.			
7.)	RHYTHMS			
	2/4			
	4/4			
	6/8			
	7/8			
	9/8 Karshlimar			
	Ayoub			
	Beledi			
	Bolero/Rhumba			
	Chiftitelli			
	Maksoom			
	Musmoody			
	Other:			
	Other:			
	Other			

8.)	RHYTHM ACC—ZILLS			
	a.) How to wear			
	b.) How to play			
	c.) What to play			
	1. Example: 4/4 (single, double, triple)			
9.)	RHYTHM ACC—TAM			
	a.) How to hold			
	b.) How to play			
	c.) What to play			
10.)	STYLE—CABARET			
	a.) Arabic			
	b.) Egyptian			
	c.) Greek/Turkish			
	d.) Other, misc.			
	e.) Costume/Venue considerations			
11.)	STYLE—ETHNIC, ETC.			
	a.) Ghawazee			
	b.) Saidy			
	c.) Other, misc.			
	d.) Costume/Venue considerations			

BEGINNER

The Beginning Belly Dance sessions cover pre-dance exercises (standing warmups); anatomy of a step (isolations); beginning dance movements (for arms, shoulders, neck, rib cage and hips); basic and specialty dance (veil & tambourine-how to use & routines); 4/4 beledi, Chiftitelli, and 9/8 rhythms, and rhythm accompaniments. The required review/self-test and dance performance at the end of the session assure both student and teacher that required lessons were learned.

INTERMEDIATE

Rather than learning many new steps, students in Intermediate classes will work with many of the basic movements from the Beginning level and will add variations to them, combine them with similar or different movements, and work on making smooth transitions from one step into another.

A. VARIATIONS: Are modifications/alterations of a basic step, for example: Hip Circle in a Circle, Basic Karshlimar with a Hop, Figure 8 with a Bounce, etc. (Usually, the variant is not a step in itself.)

B. COMBINATIONS: Join similar or different steps together, for example: Camel Walk with Rib Circle, Basic Karshlimar with a Hip Shimmy, etc. (Usually the combined step is a step that can be performed by itself.)

C. TRANSITIONS: Take you from one step into a different step, gracefully, for example: going from Hip Circle into a Walking Hip Shimmy smoothly (movements aren't "choppy" or "jerky")

ADVANCED, GROUP/TROUPE & PERFORMER

These lessons cover advanced dance movements (i.e. "challenging zill and/or step combinations); a four-part "Egyptian Oriental" dance routine; floor dancing, taxim, and sword dancing; choreography techniques and YOUR CHOREOGRAPHED ROUTINE!

Students will work toward developing their own "unique" style-as opposed to imitating their instructor's style, acknowledging the differences of distinct "Belly Dance" styles, and preparing to enter the "Belly Dance" workforce as a performer or instructor.

The required review/self-test and dance performances at the end of each session assure both student and instructor that required lessons were learned.

Chapter 2

Belly Dance Technique

Part I—Introduction

Part I—Warmup Stretches, Head/Neck, Shoulder/Arm & Rib Cage Movements

Set Goals to Achieve upon Completion of this Chapter! By the end of this chapter, you should have completed:

- Warm-up Stretches
- Head/Neck Isolations
- Basic Shoulder/Arm Movements
- Rib Cage Movements

Before moving on to Chapter 3

A. Warmup Stretches

Before you began dancing-you should prepare your body for the dance movements by doing a few minutes of warmup stretches:

1.) Six Way Body Stretch:
Bounce 4 times in each direction,
Bounce 2 times in each direction,
Hold 8 counts in each direction.

DIRECTIONS

a.) Bent over with hands behind you,

    b.) Bent over with hand below in front of you,
    c.) Leaning towards the left side w/right arm overhead,
    d.) Standing backbend w/hands in back,
    e.) Standing straight w/knees bent,
    f.) Leaning towards the right side w/left arm overhead.

2.) Upper Body Twist Stretch

Stand straight with feet slightly apart and both arms extended to sides, shoulder level, twist right arm forward to left side while twisting left arm in back; then reverse direction: twist left arm forward to right side while right arms twists back.

SIX WAY BODY STRETCH

① ② ③ ④ ⑤

⑥ REPEAT #3
(BEND TO RIGHT)

A. Pushme/Pullme

Lift left heel and bend left knee slightly, lean body towards left side, rest left hand on left hip and reach right arm upwards towards ceiling; repeat stretch on right side.

B. Anatomy of a Step

Let's take a pause from the lesson now and discuss the anatomy of a Belly Dance step. Belly Dance movements range from travel and stationary movements to isolated and multiplex movements. A good starting point for beginning students is learning how to isolate the four basic body parts:

1.) Shoulders (b, c, e)
2.) Neck (a, b, c, e)
3.) Rib Cage (a, b, c, d, e)
4.) Hips (a, d, e)

The various body parts can be moved independently "isolated" in various shapes: circle, figure 8, diamond, lines, etc. The letters in parentheses indicate some directions the basic body parts can move in:

a.) Slide (2, 3, 4)
b.) Thrust (1, 2, 3)
c.) Diamond (1, 2, 3)
d.) Half-Circle (3, 4)
e.) Circle (1, 2, 3, 4)

Also keep in mind that some movements are used basically for exercise only (i.e. rib thrusts, neck diamond, shoulder thrusts, etc.); but not for actual dance performance—this would be left up to individual taste and preference. Now, back to the movement isolations.

C.) Head/Neck Isolations:

1.) Neck Slides

To practice this one, hold both palms close to your ears, try to extend your ears to your palms without bobbing your head up or down. Remember, this movement is a straight slide from side to side.

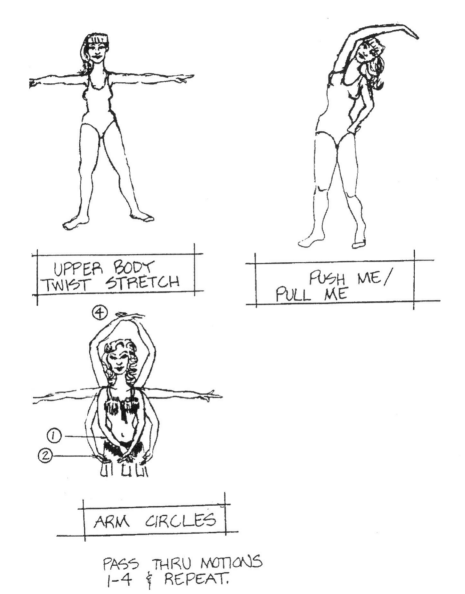

UPPER BODY
TWIST STRETCH

PUSH ME/
PULL ME

④

①
②

ARM CIRCLES

PASS THRU MOTIONS
1-4 & REPEAT.

2.) Neck Thrust

The head extends forward and back (not up or down).

3.) Neck Diamond:

This is a combination of the slides and thrusts; for example-Neck Thrust Forward, then Neck Slide to Left Side, then Neck Thrust Back, then Neck Slide to Right Side, repeat; then reverse direction.

4.) Neck Circle:

Try to think of this as a diamond with smoother edges. Start with Neck Thrust Forward, then circle to Neck Slide position on Left Side, then circle to Neck Thrust position in back, then circle to Neck Slide position on Right Side, repeat; then reverse direction.

5.) Head Roll:

Head drops forward then rolls to left side, then rolls to back (open mouth if necessary), then rolls to right side, repeat; then reverse direction. You can also warmup the head for this by doing Head Side to Side. The head goes down on the Right then Left side, for about 8 counts (or 4 counts per side). Then the head stretches forward and back for about 8 counts (4 counts front and 4 counts back). Follow this stretch with the head roll (front, side, back side).

D. Shoulder/Arm Movements

1.) Shoulder Isolation

    a.) Thrust right shoulder forward, upward, back, down, circle right shoulder, then reverse circle direction;

    b.) Thrust left shoulder forward, upward, back, down, circle left shoulder, then reverse circle direction;

    c.) Thrust both right and left shoulders in the same directions-forward, upward, back, down, circle both shoulders in the same direction, then reverse circle;

    d.) Thrust both right and left shoulder in opposite directions-forward, upward, back, down, circle both shoulders in opposite directions, then reverse circle.

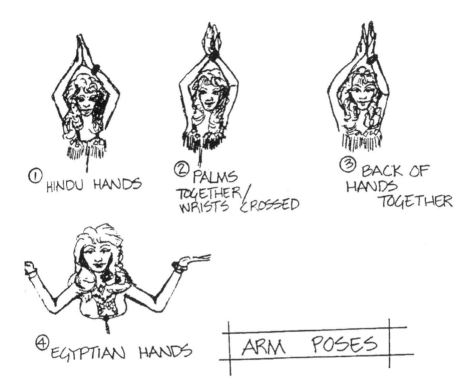

① HINDU HANDS

② PALMS TOGETHER/ WRISTS CROSSED

③ BACK OF HANDS TOGETHER

④ EGYPTIAN HANDS

ARM POSES

⑤ CLASSIC HEADACHE

2.) Snake Arms (Figure S)

    a.) *On Sides of the Body*: The base of this movement is the simultaneous/opposite shoulder circle exercise (#4 above). The shoulder blades lead, the elbow then wrist follows the same circular shape at alternate intervals. The left arm forms the top half of an "S" shape, while the right arm forms the bottom half. Slowly, the left arm lowers while the right arm comes up-now the left arm is the lower part of the "S" while the right arm is the top part. Don't forget to perform your shoulder circles while moving the arms. Variations on Snake Arms include:

    b.) *Snake Arms in Front of the Body*: Now that you've executed Snake Arms "sideways", it's a cinch to try it in front. Remember, this is the same movement, but the "S" is traced in front, rather than the sides.

    c.) *Snake Arm Solo*: Either the Right or the Left Arm traces out a Snake Arm alone. This can be to the side of the body or inverted in front of the body.

    d.) *Snake Arms on One Side*: Both the Right and the Left Arm do a Snake Arm on the Right Side of the Body. Do a Snake Arm Circle, then repeat the Snake Arms on the Left Side of the Body.

    e.) *Inverted Snake Arms*: Perform the Snake Arms with the finger tips facing inside the body. You can also stop and do poses or face frames with the movement.

    f.) *Snake Arm Circle*: Both the Right and the Left Arm do a Snake Arm from the Right to Left side of the body (or vice versa). Or trace the circle from the top to bottom of the body.

SNAKE ARMS

① ② ③ ④

SHOULDER SHIMMT

3.) Arm Circles:

   a.) *Sunrise Arms*: The arms circle UP on the sides of the body (outside), and DOWN in front of the body (inside). Although you can initiate the Sunrise Circle either on the outside or inside of the movement. One arm can also do the circle as a solo. It is nice to watch the arm travel, especially if using only one arm.

   b.) *Sunset Arms*: The arms circle DOWN on the sides of the body (outside), and UP in front of the body (inside). You can also initiate the Sunset Circle either on the outside or inside of the movement. One arm can also do the circle as a solo. It is nice to watch the arm travel, especially if using only one arm.

   c.) *Tag-Along Circle*: Both arms circle to the right, top, left, bottom areas in front of the body. Or reverse it and both arms circle to the left, top, right and bottom.

4.) Arm Poses

   a.) *Hindu Hands* (with palms together, back of hands together, or palms together wrists-crossed);

   b.) *Egyptian Hands* (with palms facing ceiling-arms out to side or in front);

   c.) *Classic Headache* (with one hand close to face and the other arm extended to side, then reverse).

A.   Shoulder Shimmy

Review shoulder isolation exercise #4, for the shoulder shimmy what you want to use is the simultaneous/opposite shoulder thrust movement (forward & back); first try it slowly, perhaps for 8 counts ; then speed it up so that you're doing 16 counts in the same time frame as 8 (double-time); shoulder shimmy is always performed in a "lady-like" manner as it IS NOT a vulgar breast shake. Try Shoulder Shimmy with a body pose (one foot in front—the other crossed over in back); also try it with different arm poses!

NECK SLIDES

LATERAL SLIDE

CENTER AXIS

① NECK THRUST

② LEFT THRUST

③

④ RIGHT THRUST

E. Rib Cage Movements

1.)   Rib Slides

In order to do this one, you need to keep you head and hips still. Isolate, or move your rib cage as far left as it can go, then move or slide your rib cage as far right as it can go, repeat several times. (HINT: Try this when you're practicing at home-put your behind against a wall to hold it still-then practice you rib slides—much easier to do when in this position, right.)

2.)   Rib Thrusts

This one is a lot easier than rib slides-you extend your rib cage as far front as you possibly can then you cave in your rib cage (as though someone hit you in the chest with a ball).

3.   Rib Diamond

This is the same as the Neck Diamond, but only you're using your rib cage instead of your neck.

4.   Rib Circle (Horizontal)

Once again, be sure to practice your rib slides, thrusts, and diamond before you try this one—it's a movement that definitely takes a lot of practice to master.

5.   Rib Circle (Vertical)

The entire body gets involved in this step. Start with one foot slightly ahead of the other, hands extended out to sides, chest slightly lowered—trace the bottom quarter of the circle first. The chest goes forward, up, back, then since you can't go any further—the only other thing you can do is shift your body so that your chest is in the same position it started in—then you start over, forward, up, back, shift. (HINT-pretend that the circle your rib cage is tracing is on the right or left side of you—and don't make the circle too big or you'll have trouble tracing it. Also, don't expect to trace a "perfect" circle—you'll probably have more of an oval or egg shape at first.)

RIB SLIDES

NOTE: DURING PRACTICE, HANDS MAY BE HELD AT HIPS TO HELP THE ISOLATION OF THE RIBS.

① EXTEND AS FAR AS POSSIBLE & LIFT UP.

② DROP RIB CAGE & CAVE-IN CHEST.

RIB THRUST

6.   Rib Waves:

These are smaller rib circles, almost just a rib thrust forward and back, but only wavier (new word?). The waves are great with Camel Walk—so "catch the waves."

7.)   Rib Lift

This one is pretty easy-you lift your rib cage on the downbeat (lift-2-3-4). Sort of, a "diagonal" push UP.

8.)   Rib Drop

This one is a little bit more difficult, but worth its weight in gold. This "earthy" movement has you dropping your rib cage on the downbeat (drop-2-3-4), but the trick is that you have to lift it before you can drop it.

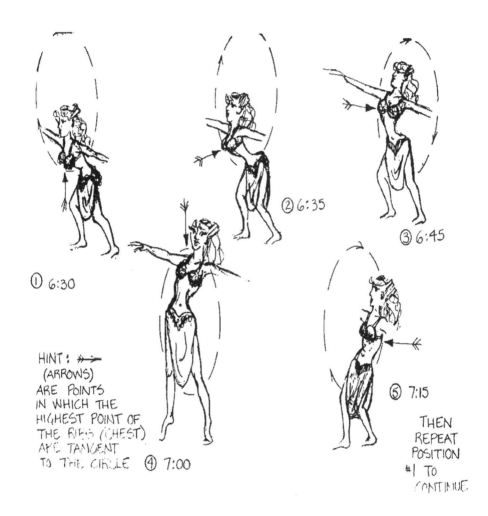

① 6:30

② 6:35

③ 6:45

④ 7:00

⑤ 7:15

HINT: ➤➤
(ARROWS)
ARE POINTS
IN WHICH THE
HIGHEST POINT OF
THE RIBS (CHEST)
ARE TANGENT
TO THE CIRCLE

THEN
REPEAT
POSITION
#1 TO
CONTINUE

Chapter 3

Slow Hipwork, Fast Hipwork, Floor Stretches, Floor Patterns, Balancing

Set Goals to Achieve upon Completion of this Chapter! By the end of this chapter, you should have completed

- Slow Hipwork
- Fast Hipwork
- Travel Movements
- Floor Patterns

Before moving on to Chapter 4

SLOW HIPWORK

A.) *Slow Hipwork*

   1.) Hip Slides

Slide or extend the right hip as far to the right as possible, then slide the left hip as far to the left as possible. (HINT-to dance with hip slides, try a "double slide" on each side".)

   2.) Hip 1/2 Circle

Pretend there is a circle on the ground directly below you—not a very—g circle or a very small circle, but a circle that is probably no more than 5 inches wider than you on all angles. You can also DRAW a circle on the sidewalk or in your backyard using chalk; or use a Hula Hoop to trace your hip circle. You're standing directly in the center of the circle—in order to—race it out, slide your right hip to the right side to get ready, then trace a half circle in back ending on the left side with the left hip extended. Then reverse, trace a half circle in back until you're back where you started with the right hip extended to the side. Then trace a half circle in front starting on the right side and ending on the left side, reverse-ending on the right side again.

3.) Hip Circle

This is like putting 2 and 2 together—you put the—half circle in back together with the half circle in front-non-stop for a continuous circle. Try doing an 8-count hip circle with 4 counts in back and 4 counts in front.

a.) *Hip Circle with a Bounce*

The hip circle part is the same but you want to add an 8-count bounce to it by putting the weight on your toes and lifting your heels (slightly) for 8 counts (doesn't have to be'8, but 8 goes well with 4/4.)

4.) Diagonal Hip Slides

Instead of doing hip slides from side to side, you angle your hips (feet stay in place) so that the right hip is in front-diagonally. Try hip slides in that position, not as easy as it sounds. Then try the same thing with the left hip in front diagonally.

5.) Figure 8 (Horizontal Infinity Loops)

Think of this as putting the diagonal hip slides together with 1/4 hip circl¼on sides. Start with the right hip in front-diagonally, slide back then circle forward with left hip, slide back with right hip, then circle forward with right hip; repeat; then reverse directions: slide forward with right hip in front, then circle back with right hip, slide forward with left hip leading, then circle back with left hip; repeat.

6.) Maya (Vertical Figure 8)

This is also an eight shape "traced" out by the hips, which is executed vertically. The circular part of this eight, travels UP on the sides of the hips, the diagonal slides DOWN are in the center of the hips.

7.) Side Camel (Reverse Vertical Figure 8)

This is a reverse "eight shape "traced" out by the hips, which is executed vertically. The circular part of this eight, travels DOWN on the sides of the hips, the diagonal slides UP are in the center of the hips.

B.) *Fast Hipwork*

1.) Hip Shimmy (Twisting)

This is similar to a washing machine agitator. The right hip twists forward, as the left hip twists back. Then reverse it and twist the left hip forward as the right hip twists back. When the right is in front, the left is in back, when the left is in front, the right is in back. The feet are about 5 inches apart, the knees are very relaxed, with only a minimal bend needed to execute the movement.

- a.) Try an 8-count Twisting Hip Shimmy in place (RLRLRLRL), then a 16 count hip shimmy in the same time frame as the 8 count (double-time).
- b.) Travel by Twisting-right foot step forward/right hip twist forward; left foot step forward/left hip twist forward; repeat. Try the walking hip shimmy in various directions (forward, left side, back, right side, square shape, diamond shape circular shape, etc.) then try the various directions in 8, 16, 24 or 32 count time intervals.

2.) Hip Shimmy (Up & Down)

Review Pre-Dance Exercise #1-straight bend. It is important to achieve this movement by elevating the pelvic at an angle. First the right up is elevated higher, then the left hip. The knees are bent and the feet flat. Don't try to cheat and get this movement by lifting the heels to elevate the hips. Use the pelvic bone and the bent knees to execute this movement. With the feet remaining flat while executing this shimmy, elevate the right knee higher than the left and therefore elevating the right hip. Next elevate the left knee higher than the right and therefore elevate the left hip. Keep alternating and picking up speed, keeping the feet flat and both knees bent as you do the up & down shimmy.

HIP   SLIDES

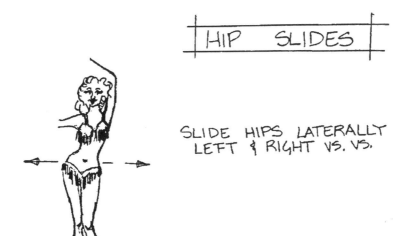

SLIDE HIPS LATERALLY
LEFT & RIGHT VS. VS.

HIP ½ CIRCLE

HINT: VISUALIZE CENTER OF
GRAVITY - BEING THE AXIS
OF CIRCLE
ONLY THE
HIP
DEVIATES

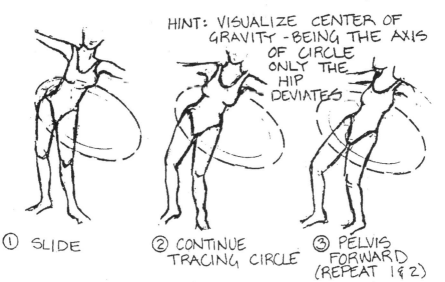

① SLIDE

② CONTINUE
TRACING CIRCLE

③ PELVIS
FORWARD
(REPEAT 1 & 2)

a.) Then try to "speed" it up "go 8" counts (RLRLRLRL) first, then try to do 16 counts in the same time frame (double-time).

b.) Travel by going Up & Down-right foot step forward/right hip lift up; left foot step forward/left hip lift up; repeat. Try directions/counts as above.

3.) Hip Thrust

a.) The *Basic Hip Thrust* is similar to a dance called the "Bump" back in the" 60's when you bump your dance partner's hips. The right hip extends to the right side, and stops sharply. You need to "lock" the right knee in order to achieve this. The left knee can be slightly bent. Reverse and do the same on the left side. a.) *Single Hip Thrusts*: alternate between the right and left side. Thrust right, left, right, left, etc.

b.) *Double Hip Thrusts*: Do 2 thrusts on the right hip, then 2 thrusts on the left hip. Repeat as needed. Also combine single and double thrusts for a really effective look: RR, LR, LL, RL, etc. This looks great when traveling in a circle.

c.) *Travel Thrust*: The right hip does a single thrust while traveling to the right. The right foot dominates as the right hip leads, the left follows (or is "dragged") by the right foot. Reverse to do the same movement traveling to the left side.

d.) *The V Thrust* is mentioned in a lot of choreographies in this book. This is a variation of a Traveling Hip Thrust. Instead of the right foot staying only to the right of the body, the right foot travels to the front right and then back right of the body, while executing the right hip thrust.

4.) Hip Lift

a.) A *Single Hip Lift* can take place with the right hip leading. The weight is on the left foot and the right heel can be elevated for a pose. Caution: Do not lift the right heel, it is only to make the movement look nice. Like the up & down hip shimmy, this movement is made possible by the knees being bent, and also elevating the pelvic bone. It is very similar to an up & down shimmy, but the difference is that one hip will lead at a time. The lead hip has to lift (then drop) in order to do more than one hip lift; the DOWNBEAT of the music determines whether you are performing hip lift or drop. If the hip is lifted during the dominant drum beats of the music, then you are doing a hip lift. If the hip is dropped during the dominant drum beats of the music, then you are doing a hip drop. Once you have the movement down, also try the hip lift with a "lean" back from the hip area. This is a classic pose.

b.) Travel with the Hip Lift to the right side. The right foot dominates as the right hip lifts, the left follows (or is "dragged") by the right foot. Reverse to do the same movement traveling to the left side.

c.) *Hip Lift in a circle*, either forward or in a backwards circle.

d.) A *Double Hip Lift* alternates the hip lift on the right and left sides: RR, LL, RR, LL, etc. This is great to travel with. The weight shifts after every other lift. Hip lift right, right (change weight), then left, left (change weight). Also try the lean back pose while doing double hip lifts.

6.) Hip Drop

a.) A *Single Hip Drop* can take place with the right hip leading. The weight is on the left foot and the right heel can be elevated for a pose. Caution: Do not drop the right heel, it is only to make the movement look nice. Like the up & down hip shimmy, this movement is made possible by the knees being bent, and also elevating the pelvic bone. It is very similar to an up & down shimmy, but the difference is that one hip will lead at a time. The lead hip has to drop (then lift) in order to do more than one hip drop; the DOWNBEAT of the music determines whether you are performing hip lift or drop. If the hip is lifted during the dominant drum beats of the music, then you are doing a hip lift. If the hip is dropped during the dominant drum beats of the music, then you are doing a hip drop. Once you have the movement down, also try the hip drop with a "lean" back from the hip area. This is a classic pose.

b.) *Travel with the Hip Drop* to the right side. The right foot dominates as the right hip drops, the left follows (or is "dragged") by the right foot. Reverse to do the same movement traveling to the left side.

c.) *Hip Drop in a Circle*, either forward or in a backwards circle.

d.) A *Double Hip Drop* alternates the hip drop on the right and left sides: RR, LL, RR, LL, etc. This is great to travel with. The weight shifts after every other drop. Hip drop right, right (change weight), then left, left (change weight). Also try the lean back pose while doing double hip drops.

C.)   Travel Movements

    1.) Travel with all Basic Movements: Review all of the movements described in Chapters 2 and 3. Perform each movement *in place* first, and then try to travel with each movement. Realize the difference between the *Basic* Movement and the *Travel* Locomotive step.

        a.) You could use *Step-Together-Step* Travel Movement in conjunction with a *Basic* Movement such a Neck Slide or Snake Arms.

        b.) You could use a *Grapevine* Travel Movement in conjunction with a Shoulder Shimmy or Hip Shimmy

HIP CIRCLE

① BEND KNEES

② SLIDE LEFT HIP

③

④

⑤

c.) You could perform a *Hip Circle* traveling to the right or left sides of the stage area, by being aware of the weight change that occurs naturally when performing a hip circle. The weight travels to the left foot (when the hip circle is traced on the left side) and to the right foot (when the hip circle is being traced on the right side of the body). When the weight is on an opposite foot (for example, the right foot), move the left foot a bit to travel. When the weight shifts to the left foot, move the right foot a bit to travel more.

d.) Don't rule out using a plain, basic *Walk*. Alone or combined with a Shoulder Shimmy or Neck Slide. Sometimes, you can have too much going on, or too many movements that look confusing. Sometimes a simple Walk, is more effective than the most contrived, layered combination of movements.

2.) Camel Walk (Front)

The foot work is: right foot step forward, left foot step in place, right step again in place forward, left foot hold 1 count. Then left foot step forward, right foot step in place, left foot step in place again forward, right foot hold 1 count. Repeat. This is a four-count movement, so don't forget to give the HOLD its one count.' a. Suggested Arm Movement-The feet lead the arms in this one-when the left foot steps forward the left arm goes out to the left side (the right arm does a pose by the face; then the arms are reversed when the right foot steps forward. b. VARIATION-Try the Camel Walk with the Rib Cage Wave (#16 above). The "wave" will be four counts also, or forward/back/forward/back.

3.) Step-Together-Step

a.) *Even*: This one is good to use when traveling from side to side. Step with the right foot to the right, then close with the left foot, Keep repeating. You can also pick up speed with this movement, especially if on the balls of your toes.

b.) *Uneven*: I usually use 3 counts for an uneven step-together-step. The footwork is right-left-right; then left-right-left. I also like to add a Figure 8 sway of the hips with this, as the weight changes from predominant right, to predominant left. The arms can follow this movement by doing a Figure 8 sway on the right, then left side.

4.) Grapevine

    a.) A *Classic* Grapevine can start by leading with the Right Foot and traveling to the Left. The right foot crosses in front of the body, the left foot steps out to the left side, the right foot crosses in back of the body, and the left foot again steps out to the left side. Repeat as needed.

    b.) *Variation 1*: Angle the body to face left, as the right foot crosses in front; and later angle the body to face right as the right foot crosses in back of the body. This is really effective when using the Grapevine to 9/8 Rhythm with Skirt Flounces.

    c.) *Variation #2*: Top your Grapevine with a Shoulder Shimmy, an Up & Down Hip Shimmy or a Hip Vibration.

FLOOR PATTERNS

D.) *Floor Patterns*

A professional dancer exudes self-confidence as she performs a variety of dance movements with finger cymbals or with a veil. One tip that has helped me in free style dancing and also with choreography is the use of Floor Patterns. Floor Patterns are a map, or the design that you trace out, as you perform in the stage area.

You'll notice in many of the choreographies contained in this book, that the routine is performed while tracing out a circle shape, a square shape, a diamond shape, etc. on the stage area.

HIP CIRCLE

① BEND KNEES

② SLIDE LEFT HIP

③

④

⑤

The use of Floor Patterns gives your dance a sense of purpose. It also can make it look as though you really know what you're doing. Dancing randomly, across the stage area or through the audience, can sometimes come across as haphazard. Or, staying in one spot for an entire dance can make you look like a beginner, who is afraid to travel across the stage.

1.) Make Good Use of Your Stage Area: Use the right and left sides, the front and back areas. The center of the stage is a very strong area, and can be used effectively for your drum solos or most dramatic movements.

2.) Give the Audience a Chance to Breath: In a 15 minute dance, you should allow enough time to communicate with the audience (looking at different audience members throughout the dance); while saving enough time to "get into" yourself. You can look up, down, over your shoulder, or at a movement you are performing. This time into yourself gives the audience a much-need time to light a cigarette or sip their drinks. Also, consider a speaker or actor who constantly "looks" at the audience or camera. Too much "dead on" contact can also be annoying.

3.) Show All Dimensions: Don't only show 'he front of your body. Shimmy with your back to the audience. Look over one shoulder. Do a hip drop with the body facing a diagonal angle. Do a vibration with the balance uneven. Show off a jewel or appliqué on back of the belt. Give them your total picture.

4.) Some Popular Floor Patterns to Trace Out:
   a.) *Square*: Start at the left front corner on a square stage. Then do an 8 count shimmy across the front, then travel to the back right corner with an 8 count shimmy, continue with an 8 count shimmy to the left back corner and end with an 8 count shimmy to return to the front left corner. Do is even more effective with an even beat rhythm like 4/4, where a 32 count phrase of music is used.
   b.) *Circle*: Start at the Center front of stage area. For a 32 count circle you would travel to the right side for 8 counts, do the center back for 8 counts, the left side for 8 counts and end up center front with the last 8 counts. Adjust the counts for a 16 or 64 count circle pattern.
   c.) *Eight*: Start in the center of the stage and trace out a large eight shape on the right side of the stage. This could be 8, 16 or 32 counts. Finish the left part of the eight shape with the remaining 8, 16 or 32 counts for the musical phrase. This is great to use with Walking Hip Shimmy.

d.) *Diamond*: Similar to the Circle, but with sharp edges. Start at the Center front of stage area. For a 32 count diamond you would travel to the right side for 8 counts, do the center back for 8 counts, the left side for 8 counts and end up center front with the last 8 counts. Adjust the counts for a 16 or 64 count diamond pattern.

e.) *Triangle*: You could start at the Right/Front part of stage area, then travel to the Left/Front, Center/Back and return to the Right/Front; or vice versa. An inverted Triangle, could start at the Right/Back part of the stage area, then travel to the Left/Back, Center/Front and return to the Right/Back area; or vice versa. Play with starting the Triangle at different parts of the pattern.

HIP CIRCLE

① BEND KNEES

② SLIDE LEFT HIP

③

④

⑤

FLOOR STRETCHES

1. FLOOR BOUNCE: You are sitting on behind with legs arranged in a "V" shape in front of you (doesn't matter to me whether your toes are pointed or straight—pointing my toes sometimes gives me cramps). From this position, bounce your chest area (carefully) on the right thigh 4 times, the center 4 times, the left thigh 4 times and the center 4 times; then bounce on the right thigh 2 times, the center 2 times, the left thigh 2 times, and the center 2 times; and finally "hold" 8 counts on the right thigh, 8 counts in the center, 8 counts on the left thigh, and 8 counts in the center.

2. BUTTERFLY: Basically the same position as above, only you will bend the knees and brings toes in toward your body. From this position bounce 4 times to right side, 4 times in center, 4 times to left side, and 4 times in center; then "hold" 4 counts on right side, 4 counts in center, 4 counts on left side and 4 counts in center.

3. THIGH SLIDE: A variation to the above positions, extend the left leg out towards your left side and put the right leg in back-using a bent knee to accomplish that. From this position bounce 4 times to left side, 4 time over left knee, and 4 times towards right side; "hold" 4 counts on left side, 4 counts over left knee, and 4 times towards right side; last of all "hold" 8 counts with upper body "laying" down in back; TRY EVERYTHING AGAIN-REVERSED ON THE RIGHT SIDE.

4. BERBER STRETCH: This time you are on your knees—from that position, extend or "slide" the right leg out in front of you—pull it back in and then extend or "slide" the left leg out in front of you.

5. BACKBEND STRETCH: Again, on knees, try a half backbend—keep working at it until you can do a full backbend from knees and go into "floor position" and come up again.

6. HINGE STRETCH: While still on knees—keep your upper body straight and lean backward, try this with thighs together 8 times and with thighs apart 8 times.

7. HIP MOVEMENT STRETCH: Try any hip movement from the "knee position": hip circle, maya, side camel, figure 8, "up & down" shimmy, hip slide, etc.

FLOOR DANCING

1.) Snake in Basket

Can be performed standing or on knees, begin with a hip circle, then make a smooth transition into a rib cage circle; another variation is to perform the hip circle on knees—lowering until you are sitting, then perform the rib circle sitting—raising yourself until you're on your knees again.

2.)   Body Turn #1

Begin by sitting on both calves with knees bent in front of you, then sit on bent knees and legs on left side, then sit with knees up in front, then sit with bent knees and legs on left side. Do an arm circle or snake arms with the turn. Try the turn in both directions, using smooth transitions.

3.)   Body Turn #2

Start in the same position as Turn #1 above, then slide the left hand and extend entire body to left side (keeping head erect as though something were on top of it and left leg bent), roll around to front with entire body extended flat against floor (with head erect), then roll to right side-sliding right hand out first-bending right leg-and keeping head erect. Also try this movement while balancing a cane or sword on your head.

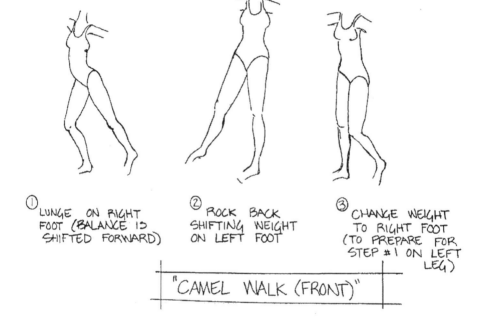

① LUNGE ON RIGHT FOOT (BALANCE IS SHIFTED FORWARD)

② ROCK BACK SHIFTING WEIGHT ON LEFT FOOT

③ CHANGE WEIGHT TO RIGHT FOOT (TO PREPARE FOR STEP #1 ON LEFT LEG)

"CAMEL WALK (FRONT)"

4.)   Hinge

Same as Hinge Stretch, but this time we will add variants to it. First of all try a hip shimmy going back then coming forward, next try a hip vibration, then try a shoulder shimmy, next try it with snake arms only, and last of all try it with a vibration going back with a rib undulation coming forward. The possibilities are endless.

5.)   Hip Movements

Any hip movement can be performed standing or on your knees, because your hips do the isolating—not your feet or knees. Try them all on your knees: Hip Circle, Figure 8, Maya, Side Camel, Hip Shimmy, Hip Thrust, etc. Add various arm movements (Snake Arms, Arm Circle, etc.) and you have a wide possibility of floor movements.

6.)   Berber Walk

Start on both knees, then extend the left knee forward as far forward as it will go—keep sliding until the knee completely touches; the ground; next slide the right knee forward and up and then extend it as far forward as it will go until the knee completely touches the ground; do 1 or 2 complete Berber Walks or keep repeating. Use this with various arm movements and/or with a cane or sword balanced on your head.

7.)   Veil Movements

You can incorporate veil into floor dancing. One of my favorites is the start with veil swirls-standing, and continue doing veil swirls while lowering your knees. Once on your knees you could do any hip movement, Berber Walk, hinge, etc. with the veil framing the body—or, you could continue the swirls while going into Body Turn #2, do a pose while lying on the floor with back and head on ground and knees bent at your sides. Make sure the veil is draping your stomach—then go into Belly Rolls or Flutters.

8.)   Side Pose

Make a smooth transition from any knee position and/or Body Turn# or #2-then lie on your left hip with the weight on your left hip, left thigh and left hand or elbow. From this position you can do a Rib Undulation, Belly Rolls or Flutters, Arm Circles using the right arm, or a Crawl scooting forward with the left hip. You can also try this movement with a cane or sword balanced on your head.

Feel free to practice the floor dance movements in a choreographed routine using Sword. You can practice doing the floor movements only, and later add the sword if you'd like.

BALANCE TECHNIQUES

1. GETTING STARTED
    a. Your body posture is very important when it comes to balancing any prop—whether it's a cane, sword, basket, or candle, etc. Basically you will keep the head "straight", eyes forward, no "bobbing" up or down or sideways. Try it with a book on your head in an area where you are not afraid of damaging anything, i.e. a basement or rec room with carpeting or a rug.
    b. With the book on your head, try the following:
        1. Walking around the room-forward, backwards, in a circle, fast, slow, on toes, with knees bent, etc.
        2. Simple isolations of hip (the easiest to do) i.e. hip shimmy (in place or traveling), hip circle, figure 8, etc.
        3. Isolations of the rib area, i.e. rib circle, wave, shimmy, etc.
        4. Isolations/combinations of rib & hip area, also try arm circles and turns.

"CAMEL WALK"

① STEP   ② BALL   ③ CHANGE

REPEAT #1 WITH
RIGHT LEG

NOTE: ARM EXTENDS STRAIGHT
OUT WITH LEADING LEG.

2.   BALANCING A CANE

Now that you, done that—it's time to try it with an actual "prop", the cane.

Before we do that—let's think about what cane dancing consists of-3 basic elements are:

1.   Steps involving the cane,
2.   Twirls (or other movements especially for the cane),
3.   Balancing

We will cover the first two elements later in the routine, but right now let's discuss balancing.

You can balance a cane on various parts of your body—some of the most common areas used are: HEAD, HIP, SHOULDER, CHEST, AND KNEE; but before balancing the cane on any of those areas it would be wise to locate the "Balance Point" on the cane itself—once you have found it using your hands—go ahead and try placing the cane on each of the 5 areas above. However, while dancing—one cannot simply "place" the cane on the area to be balanced—it is proper to "dance" the cane there, don't just STOP DANCING—continue dancing, use a hip shimmy or vibration to distract the audience, and possible even turn your back to the audience to maintain concentration.

CONCENTRATION IS THE KEY when it comes to balancing a prop!

For another challenge, try the Choreography to *The Sword Dance*! In the Intermediate Dance section.

Chapter 4

Veil Dance

Part I: VEIL DRAPES

Set Goals to Achieve upon Completion of this Chapter! By the end of this chapter, you should have completed

- Veil Drapes
- Veil Dancing
- Veil Undrapes
- Beyond Veils

Before moving on to Chapter 5

A. What is *"Veil Dancing"* and what can it consist of?

Veil Dancing is a slow dance performed with a prop (veil or cape) usually during the second song of a routine. Veil Dancing may consist of these four elements:

1.) Draping
2.) Undraping
3.) Veil Dancing
4.) Discarding

   a. DRAPING: Is done offstage-minutes before the actual routine begins. The drape or "veil wrap" the dancer uses will be dependent on the type/style of veil (or cape), type of routine, style, level of dance, and length of routine.

A "Basic Veil Wrap" involves folding the veil over the left arm (or right); tucking the short edges into the belt on the right hip (front & back); and tucking the edge near the bust area into the right Bra strap. This veil wrap could be used with a straight (rectangular), ½ circular, or ¾ circular veil; or any combination of straight & circle veils; is suitable for cabaret or ethnic style routines, beginning-advanced dancers, and any veil dance song at least 2 minutes long.

"BASIC VEIL WRAP"

1. DRAPE VEIL OVER LEFT ARM.

2. TUCK SHORT EDGES (FRONT & BACK) INTO BELT.

3. TUCK UNDER BRA STRAP.

An "Egyptian-style Drape" involves gathering the veil length-wise and wrapping it around your neck; grabbing the two edges in back and either tucking them into the right and left belt edges (on side) or criss-crossing them first before tucking into same edges. This wrap is most suitable with straight veils, but you could also try it with a circular veil. Intermediate-Advanced dancers will find this drape a "must" for those "Oriental-style" cabaret routines with a short slow taxim/veil song.

b.) UNDRAPING: It doesn't take much sense to figure out that how you undrape is determined by how you drape. Undraping (or "dancing the veil off") is usually done during the actual performance to the 2nd song in a routine. Of course, there are exceptions to that rule. Veil undraping is not to be rushed into-rather, the veil is "danced off" gracefully, slowly and subtly using an assortment of slow movements, drapes, poses, tents, canopies, and turns. During this section of the veil dance-the veil is either fully or partially attached to the body. Attitude is extremely important here—as this is authentic middle eastern dancing-not stripping!

c. VEIL DANCING: Is an extension of the "undraping" and consists of various turns, spins, poses, swirls, tents, etc. performed with the veil completely unattached from the body.

d.) DISCARDING: The last, but not least important part of the veil dance. The object here is to get rid of the veil in timely, professional, entertaining manner.

    1.) Plain Discard: After performing a veil turn or pose, gracefully place the veil in an area of the stage that you won't use (veils are slippery sometimes, so you don't want to step on it).

VEIL — FRONT
TO BACK

VEIL DANCING

2.) Overhead Flip: Start with the veil in front of the body and dance to the back of the stage area, then flip the veil completely overhead and drop it behind you. Instead of dropping the veil you could also hold the veil in back, and do a backbend pose for a dramatic effect. This Veil Flip could also be performed on an elevated stage area. Again, you could flip the veil behind you (by having your back to the audience); or you could start with the veil in back and then flip it in front of the body.

3.) Veil Turban: Turban someone in the audience by gathering and wrapping the veil around their head-you could also get them up to dance with you (part of a Sultan Act).

B.) *Type of Veils used in Belly Dance*

1.) Straight (Rectangular) Veil: Usually 2½-3 yards of fabric in a 45, 54 or 36 inch width. Can be in chiffon, tissue lame, satin, or any other fabric that flows easily and matches or coordinates with your costume. Hemming all four edges is suggested as it makes it easier to grab the veil edges. Also, sequin or other trim is recommended for either top and/or side edges of veil as this helps you to grab the veil easier.

2.) Circular Veils: This can be a half circle, a full circle or a ¾ circle veil in the same fabric listed above. You can experiment with the same pattern used for your skirt to help in cutting out a circular shape. A half circle veil resembles a half-moon as the name suggests and can be easily cut from fabric that is 54 inches or wider. Or, if using 36 or 45 inch fabric, you may want to make the shape from 2 even pieces of fabric. A full circle veil can also be made easier to work with by putting a slit in the back panel. You might also consider adding fabric ties to the front of the veil to hold the veil until you're ready to undrape it.

a.) A ¾ Circle Veil can be easily made from 3 and ¾ yards of fabric with each panel being 1¼ yards. I've made many ¾ circle veils using the same circular shape from my skirt pattern. Also experiment with using different color panels. For example, each panel could be a different shade of blue (dark blue, medium blue and light blue). I've also made a veil using red, orange and gold panels.

FRAME FACE

VEIL DANCING

POSES

TENT

3.) Capes: This can be custom made to match your skirt, or you can make one in gold, silver or black to go with a variety of different costumes. Capes are usually distinguished from a large circle veil by being attached at the neck. Capes can range from 5 to 15 yards of fabric, most with a circular shape. For ease in use, you could also attach a fabric ties to the front of the veil to hold the veil until you're ready to undrape it. There is also a popular cape used by Belly Dancers that was inspired by the famous dancer, **Loie Fuller**. The sticks (or wooden dowels help to manipulate the 15 yards of fabric. Make them "fly" using the sticks inserted or attached via upper arm via bands. You can also try double cape work, just like double veil work and use capes with 2 different contrasting fabrics & colors (i.e. one lace the other tissue lame or pleated lame).

4.) Experiment with your Veils or Capes to make them unique! I have attached jewels, appliqués and/or extra sequin paillettes to veils. I have added metallic fringe to my orange circular veil. Also play with the hem or bottom part of the veil. You can also create a cape that has several panels with metallic fringe attached. The panels have pointed edges, as opposed to circular edges. You wouldn't want to end up with a collection of veils that all look the same. Or a lot of veils that are the same shape or have the same hem, trim or edging.

5.) Use Two or More Veils or Capes for a Special Effect. A choreographed routine for Double Veil is in the *Amayaguena* Routine).

"EGYPTIAN-STYLE DRAPE"

C.) *Beyond Veils*

1.) Boas: A feather or marabou boa can be used instead of a veil.
2.) Fans: A wide variety of fans can be used in place of a veil dance. Fans are available custom-made to match your costume in different colors or fabric bases, different sizes are available, or choices (lace, paper, plastic) to please any budget.
3.) Scarves: Substitute 2 scarves in place of double veils. This is a great look and it's usually something different.
4.) Harem Veils: These really convey the "Harem" look. I use a Face (Harem) Veil attached to a Pillbox Hat in the 2nd dance scene in my video. This is a Red/Gold Costume performing to Sultan's Dream music.
5.) Veils Used with Other Props: I use Veil with Sword, Veil with Cane, you can also use Veil with Baskets, etc.

D.) *Turns used for Veil Dancing*

1.) Push Turn: Both feet propel the body around in a turn at the same time. You can really pick up a lot of speed with the turn, especially on toes or in heels.
2.) Pedal Turn: One foot stays stationary (for example the right foot), while the other foot pivots the body around (for example the left turn). In this example you would most likely turn to the right (a forward turn).
3.) Spotting: Borrow this technique from your ballet class, by focusing on an object at eye level in the room (i.e. door window or picture); keep looking at this object while the body continues to turn. The eyes stay focused on this object, even as the head is forced to turn with the body, when the head is forced to turn with the rest of the body, snap the head around, but immediately began looking at the object again when the head finishes.

E.) *Dancing with the Veil*: I usually hold my veil with the thumb (skin) behind the veil (closer to the body) and the finger next to the thumb in front of the body. This makes it easier to hold the veil when wearing finger cymbals. The veil is held shoulder-width apart, not too tight, with a bit of flexibility so that it doesn't look stressed. Make sure the fingers holding the veil look relaxed, not stiff. The veil dance is usually performed to slow music and should look relax.

1.) Veil Turn: The veil can be in front of the body or behind you. You can turn either to your left or right. You simply hold the veil in front of the body or in back of the body. The motion of your body turning makes the veil do all the work.

2.) Veil Swirl: You can swirl to the Right (right, top, left, bottom); or Left (left, top, right, bottom). The arms trace a circle around the body. Also try the veil swirl standing still or while turning.

    a.) Swirl the same Direction: The veil swirl and the body turn both start to the left side (or right).

    b.) Swirl the opposite Direction: This is a bit more dramatic. The veil swirl goes to the left, while the body turns to the right. To reverse, the veil swirls to the right, while the body turns to the left.

3.) Veil Flounce: A dramatic, sweeping motion where the Right (or Left) hand traces out a circle of 8 shape with the veil. A Flounce can be small (on the right or left side) with both arms shoulder level or lower. To make a big flounce, have the Right hand above the head, while the left arm does a big "circle" with the veil, sweeping to the right side, front, then left side.

4.) Matador: This looks like a one-dimensional veil swirl performed in front of the body. Instead of going to the right, top, left and bottom; the veil only travels from the right to left side in front of the body. Make your Matador Turn dramatic by adding a Veil Turn as the veil rests on the left or right side.

    a.) Or, add a One-Arm Vertical Circle Flip, using the veil on one side of the body with one arm. The right arm circles forward, down, back and up; while the left arm rests on the right shoulder

Shalimar with the 18 Yard Cape in Seattle, WA

5.) One Arm Veil: Practice this with fabric that can "catch" the air. Tissue lame or satin works best. Start with the veil in back of the body, then gather it more on the right side (so that you won't have excess fabric to slip on). You can then try either a Veil Turn or an Airplane Turn with the Veil in back, using only one arm. You'd be surprised at how easy this is to do once you practice it a few times. The secret is using the right fabric, gathering the excess fabric and also turning your body fast enough so that you don't step on any fabric that touches the floor.

    a.) I like to end up my One Arm Veil Turn with a Lasso Turn. The Lasso is actually a One-Arm Veil Swirl that goes in front and back of the body

6.) Airplane Turns: The body executes a "Barrel-like" turn while the arms holding the veil go up and down, like an airplane propeller. I like to purposely hold the veil very tight when doing airplane turns. Also, make sure your arms (airplane propellers) execute even counts (i.e. up-2-3, down-2-3). The veil can be held in front of the body or in back of the body. You can also do an airplane turn with the veil draped around the neck.

7.) Veil Frames & Tents:

    a.) Frame Eyes or Face: The veil is in front of the body. Make sure no fingers are peeking out when you bring the veil up to frame your face, or eyes. The hands can also be joined, palms together. This looks great with Neck Slide or Eye Slides.

    b.) Frame Ribs or Belly: The veil is in front of the body lowered to the stomach or rib cage area. Or you could have it partially tucked in the belt to frame these areas. You can show off your Belly Rolls or Rib Circles with the frame.

    c.) Frame Hips: The veil is in front of the body, lowered to the hip area. You can show off your hip shimmies, Maya or Side Camel with this frame. If using 2 veils (one in front and one in back), you can also *step out* of the veil at this point.

    d.) Veil Tent: The veil is in back of the body, usually overhead. Open and close the tent for a dramatic effect. You can also enclose your BellyGram recipient inside the tent and whisper Happy Birthday. Or, you can do a floor pose by closing the tent and lowering yourself to the floor for a dramatic effect.

Chapter 5

Rhythm Accompaniments

Part I: The Naturals

Set Goals to Achieve upon Completion of this Chapter! By the end of this chapter, you should have completed . . .

- How to wear Finger Cymbals
- How to play Finger Cymbals
- What to Play
- Using Tambourines or other Natural Rhythm Accompaniments

Before moving on to Chapter 6

A. Natural Rhythm Accompaniments:

Have you ever noticed someone clapping their hands (or snapping their fingers) at a party while dancing? They were providing a "Rhythm Accompaniment" to the music or beat. Belly Dancers also use various "Rhythm Accompaniments" while dancing, including: Finger Cymbals, Tambourines, Drums (strapped to body) and Coins. You can control the first three, or play beats to certain rhythms; but the coins cannot be controlled-although they do add sound to your performance.

Before you can learn how to play the finger cymbals or tambourine, it is a good idea to review playing your "natural" accompaniments: hands & fingers.

1.) *HAND CLAPPING*: A good song to start with is "*Raks Leyla*" because its 4/4 time rhythm is easy to work with: Clap 12345678. Then try walking and clapping at the same time: Clap/Walk 12345678 (RLRLRLRL). Then try clapping with the Walking Hip Shimmy step: Clap/Shimmy Walk 12345678 (RLRLRLRL). Now try to do the entire song while clapping (during some parts you'll need to Clap 1234-pause, 1234-pause (RLRL, LRLR); but basically-it's 12345678 all the way! (This is a good way to prepare for Tambourine Dancing.)

2.) *FINGER SNAPPING*: This one is more difficult to do than Hand Clapping-but it will prepare you more for Finger Cymbals. Still using "*Raks Leyla*" Snap 12345678 (RLRLRLRL). Then try walking and snapping at the same time: Snap/Walk 12345678. Then try snapping with the Walking Hip Shimmy step: snap/Shimmy Walk 12345678. Are you using the right hand with the left foot or the right hand with the right foot when you walk? Try to find which way works best for you.

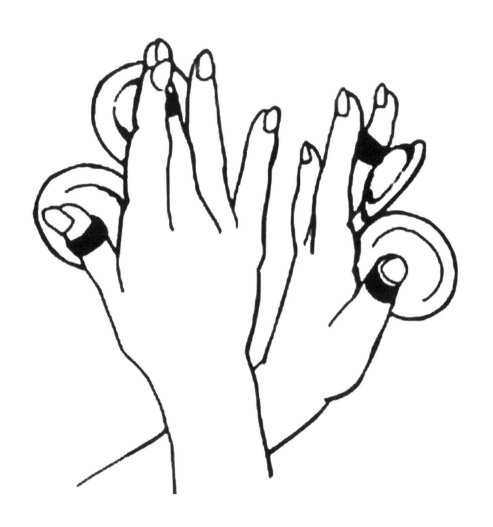

B.) *Finger Cymbals (Zills)* to Accompany Rhythm

Zills, also **zils** or **finger cymbals,** (from *Turkish zil,* "cymbals") are tiny metallic *cymbals* used in *belly dancing* and similar performances. They are called *sājāt* (تاجاص) in *Arabic.* They are similar to *Tibetan tingsha bells.* [*Source*: Wikipedia]

1.) **How to wear**

  a.) Belly Dancers use 4 cymbals (2 pairs), which are worn on the thumb and middle fingers.

2.) **How to play**

  a.) This four-piece "noise-maker" works by "hitting" the edges of the two cymbals held in one hand, then "hitting" the edges of the two cymbals held in the other hand (i.e. first "hit" the cymbals together in the right hand; then "hit" the cymbals together in the left hand—don't hit the cymbals together in both hands at the same time—unless you are doing so for special emphasis).

3.) **What to play**

  a.) *Clack*

    1. Hitting the cymbals on the thumb and middle finger of the same hand; then hitting the cymbals on the thumb and middle finger of the other hand, for example:
    2. HIT: Right (hand), Left (hand), Right (hand); then Left (hand), Right (hand), Left (hand). The result should be a noise that sounds something like a "clack", this is the most common method of playing finger cymbals.

  b.) *Click*

    1. Gently click the edges of the thumb cymbal to the middle finger cymbal for a softer, quieter sound. This gentle "click" is effective to use for special effects or during your floor work or taxim part of the dance routine.

c.) *Trill*

1. Holding both cymbals edges (of one hand) together loosely then shaking those edges until you get the effect of a "tingle" or bell.
2. TINGLE: Shake (tingle) right hand cymbals only for about 8 counts; then shake (tingle) left hand cymbals only for about 8 count; then see if you could tingle both hands together at the same time!

d.) *Mute*

1. This resembles a clamshell. Clicking the edges of the cymbals on the right hand then clicking the edges of the cymbals on the left hand (you can maintain control of the cymbals by somewhat "holding" the back part of the cymbal with your four fingers then your fingers can "meet" the edge of the cymbal on the thumb; you could also reverse this procedure by "holding" the thumb cymbal securely, then use it to "meet" the edge of the cymbal held loosely in place by the four fingers.
2. CLICK: Right (hand), Left (hand), Right (hand); then Left (hand), Right (hand), Left (hand).

FINGER CYMBAL BASICS

Put below knuckle on middle fingers & thumbs

1.) How to play (basic normal sound, tingle, soft muted sound, loud clack sound)
2.) SINGLE TIME:
1 2 3 4 5 6 7 8
3.) DOUBLE TIME:
12, 34, 56, 78, 9-10, 11-12, 13-14, 15-16
4.) TRIPLE TIME: 123, pause, 123, pause, etc. Try Slow or Half Time 1st:
123, 123, 123, 123, 123, 123, 123, 123
5.) BELEDI: 1-2, pause, 1; 1-2, pause, 1, etc.:
1-2, 1; 1-2, 1; 1-2, 1; 1-2, 1

6.) **Know which rhythm to use for particular dance songs**
a.) Some *Basic* Rhythms. There are many different rhythms used for Middle Eastern Dancing: Beledi, Musmoody, 9/8

Karshlimar, Chiftitelli, Bolero, Rhumba, 7/8, 6/8 (Persian, Iraqi, Moroccan), Ayoub, 2/4, Zar, Saidi, etc.

b.) Become knowledgeable with commonly-used rhythms. Read the back of album, tape or CD covers to find out which rhythms were used on the tape.

c.) Note the differences between certain rhythms. Beledi will have 2 strong drum beats, immediately followed by one single drum beat. Compared to Musmoody, which will have 2 strong drum beats, a pause, and then one single drum beat. In all cases, listen for the strongest drum beats and the pattern they follow. In many middle eastern songs, there will be a *dominant* drummer or drum beat playing the main rhythm (i.e. Beledi, Musmoody, 7/8, etc. ; but there might also be an additional or *secondary* drummer or drum beats that are adding to or **embellishing** the main rhythm. The "fill-in" beats or **embellishments** offer an opportunity to layer shimmies on a main movement or add fill-in beats to your finger cymbals.

d.) Note how the *musical phrasing* of the music affect the rhythm. There might be a song that has a steady beat that sounds like a 4/4 rhythm. You might listen to this song and think, oh, I bet that is 4/4 rhythm because I can hear the drum steadily going boom, boom, boom, boom, boom, boom, boom, boom. But, then you might listen closer to the song and hear how the main instrument plays the **melody** line. If a vocal, the singer might repeat a musical phrase after only 4 counts; or if an instrumental song, the melody line might be repeated every 4 counts. This song might be a 2/4 meter rather than a 4/4 rhythm. Check the song liner notes to compare. Or, try to find another version of this song in your tape library to verify the name of the rhythm.

e.) After doing research on names of rhythms contained in the music you already have and listening to the different rhythms, set a goal to *memorize* or be able to **distinguish** between the rhythms. You might recognize one song a 4/4 rhythm, but you might hear that 9/8 karshlimar was used as the finale for this routine. Keep testing yourself until you have memorized at least 5 different rhythms that you can name and also play finger cymbals to.

f.) More on the subject of using different *versions* of the same song. This can be an effective tool in learning and memorizing rhythm. Start noticing the names of songs that you have on several different belly dance tapes. Some of these songs may be classic favorites, like *Raks Leyla, Rampi Rampi, Ah Ya Zain*, etc. Match the names with the rhythms and make a note of it for yourself. This is helpful if you are performing with live music for the first time and the band asks you which songs to play. The band might not be familiar with all the different songs you have in your personal tape library. What if the band didn't buy the same tapes as you, and won't be familiar with your tape that has *Bedouin Wedding* on it? But, you can't go wrong if you request that the band play certain **rhythms** instead. If you did your research and knew that all the songs in your library named *Rampi Rampi* were always a 9/8 karshlimar; then you had already rehearsed some steps and finger cymbal patterns to 9/8 karshlimar, then you might request that this band end your routine with a 9/8 karshlimar. It might not be *Rampi Rampi*, they may only be familiar with *Marinella* or *Tomzara*, which are 2 other versions of a 9/8 karshlimar song. But since 9/8 is still 9/8, you could get by with using the same dance movements and finger cymbal patterns—even though there could be differences in the musical phrasing and melody line.

5.) Finally, to use finger cymbals effectively as a rhythm accompaniment, you must learn to:
    a. Play the cymbals alone (Clack, Click, Tingle, Mute, etc.)
    b. Play the cymbals while moving-walking, dancing
    c. Hold the cymbals while performing a veil dance
    d. Learn the various rhythms used in Belly Dance; and
    e. Learn the various finger cymbals patterns used with those Belly Dance rhythms!

Finger Cymbal Pattern:	*1*	*2*	*3*	*4*	*5*	*6*	*7*	*8*
1.) 4/4 (Triple Time)	R L R 1 2 3	L R L 1 2 3	R L R 1 2 3	L R L 1 2 3	R L R 1 2 3	L R L 1 2 3	R L R 1 2 3	L R L 1 2 3
2.) Beledi	R 1	L 2			R 1			
3.) 9/8 Karshlimar	R 1		L 2		R 3		R L R 1 2 3	

There are many rhythms in belly dancing music that can be spelled out in finger cymbal playing: [*Source*: Wikipedia]

- triplets (left/right/left/pause—"giddyup, giddyup, giddyup")
- quads (L/R/L/R/no pause)
- beledi (dum/dum/tek-a-tek/dum-tek-a-tek)
- chiftatelli (dum/dum/tek-a-tek/dum/dum/dum—"John went to the sea; caught. three. fish.")
- ayub (dum/a-tek-tek—"buy more shoes, and . . . buy more shoes, and . . . ,")
- bolero (dum/tek-a-tek-tek/dum/dum/dum/dum—"I want to be a belly dancer")

B.   The Tambourine

Right-handed students will find that holding the tambourine in the right hand and "hitting" it (gently) on the left palm works best (opposite hand for left-handed students). Again, using parts of *"Raks Leyla"* choreography: Hit 12345678. Then try walking and hitting at the same time: Hit/Walk 12345678 (RLRLRLRL). And last but, not least-try the Walking Hip Shimmy while hitting the tambourine.

1.   Suggested Costume for a Tambourine Dance:
   a.)   Ethnic Style: Harem Pants with sleeved vest, bolero and accent panels or accent skirt; coined bra, belt & jewelry
   b.)   Cabaret Style: Turkish-ruffled skirt (or Accent Skirt) with sleeved vest, bolero and beaded bra, belt & jewelry.

You might want to use a lot of fringe, perhaps the colors red, black and/or green to achieve a "Gypsy" look for either cabaret or ethnic style.

D.)   *Other Rhythm Accompaniments*

Hand clapping, finger cymbals and tambourines are only a start. Explore other possibilities, like maracas and. You can also in some cases use your **cane** as a rhythm accompaniment, by tapping the straight (not hooked) cane end on the stage floor. The rhythm of your song could be tapped along with the music, for example, if you were performing cane dance to a Beledi rhythm, then you could set aside part of this song to tap the Beledi rhythm with the Cane (1-2, 1, 1-2, 1), etc.

Chapter 6

Dance Choreographies

Dance Level Checklist

1. ***Beginning Belly Dance***: Warmup stretches (standing), isolations for shoulders, neck, rib cage, hips, etc.; basic movements for above areas, use of basic movements in a simple dance routine, veil dancing (drapes, turns, body frames, discarding, multiple veilwork, or a choreographed routine for soloist), finger cymbals (how to play, basic rhythms and dance movements for 4/4, beledi, chiftitelli, and slow 9/8), choreographed tambourine dance to 9/8 karshlimar rhythm;

2. ***Intermediate Belly Dance***: Standing and/or Floor stretches, continuation of basic isolations and/or movements for shoulders, neck, rib cage, and hips—including combinations, variations and transitions from one to another, cane dancing—how to balance, steps for, and a choreographed routine, group dances to candle, drum solo and veil dance, continuation of finger cymbals—drills in single/double/triple time, ayoub, musmoody, introduction to dance styles and showmanship for performers;

3. ***Advanced Belly Dance***: Standing, Floor stretches and Floor Dance, Slow Taxim, advanced zill/step combinations and variations, cabaret dance routines to include veil/cape intro, stage dance, taxim, drum solo, finale, finger cymbals to iraqi, persian or moroccan 6/8, 7/8, bolero, ayoub and faster 9/8, continuation of dance styles (egyptian, greek, arabic, etc.) and emphasis on developing one's own style/technique, belly dance history, business and costuming, working with musical phrasing and introduction to choreography, group or solo dances using sword, tambourine, canes;

4. ***Troupe/Group Dance***: Choreographed routines to 4/4, drum solo, veil, beledi, ghawazee, 9/8; use of props—cane, tambourine, sword, candle, veil, etc., forming a troupe, tips & traps, ethnic & cabaret costuming, floor patterns for groups of 2, 3, 4, etc.
5. ***Performers***: Costuming, showmanship, and business, putting together a stage show, working with musical phrasing, choreography vs. free style, dance styles & technique, ethnic & cabaret dance styles, floor patterns for stage, choreography assignment.

DANCE CHOREOGRAPHY ASSIGNMENTS

Beginning Level
1. Raks Leyla, cabaret with finger cymbals to 4/4
2. Jasmine Dancer, cabaret w/veil and finger cymbals
3. Varter, veil dance
4. Bedouin Wedding, cane dance to beledi
5. Tomzara, tambourine dance to 9/8

Intermediate Level
1. Ambera, cabaret w/cape entrance
2. Tamzara, group tambourine dance to 9/8
3. Amayaguena/El Porompompero, Spanish double veil w/drum solo finale
4. The Sword Dance
5. Kalamatiano, skirt dance to 7/8

Advanced Level
1. Bahia
2. Zannube, 4-Part Cabaret
3. Welcome to the Dance, YaSalaam Drum Solo, Finale
4. Uskudar, Turkish cabaret w/finger cymbals
5. Ro-He cape entrance, Baladi Thriller, Drum Solo, Finale

Group Level
1. Hanna Drumzilzia, drum solo w/finger cymbals
2. A Whole New World, group veil dance
3. Phaedra Pharonica, pharonic candle dance
4. I Remember Egypt, sword dance
5. Yahlewa, Canes, Tambourine & Zills

Performer Level

1. Dance Ramza/Selma/Nazira, cabaret entrance, veil & finale
2. Sahara City, veil or cape entrance w/finger cymbals
3. Badia, Egyptian Cabaret
4. Faqset el Fadaa, Veil, stage dance, finale
5. Rugisnee, cape dance, Yani drum solo
6. Assignment: Choreograph a 5-Part Dance Routine that is 8-10 Minutes Long

BEGINNER DANCES

Beginner Dance #1

RAKS LEYLA, 4/4 Beledi w/Chiftitelli
Choreographed in 1984, music by George Abdo, *The Joy of Belly Dancing*

NOTE:

This dance can be performed as a solo, duet or group of 4 dancers.

The instructions are written for the dancer(s) on the Left side of stage who are leading with their right foot.

A group of 4 dancers would have a dancer on R front, R back, L front & L back. The dancers on Left side lead with right foot and the dancers on the Right side lead with their left foot, until they switch sides and use the opposite lead foot.

1. Intro 16 counts (Hip drop pose in place)
2. Walking hip shimmy 32 cts. (in square, 8 cts. on each side, R foot leads)
3. Neck slide pose 8 cts. (4 cts. on R, 4 cts. on L)
4. Shoulder shimmy pose 8 cts. (4 cts. on R, 4 cts. on L)
5. Turn 8 cts. (from stage L to stage R)
6. Walking hip shimmy 32 cts. (in square, 8 cts. on each side, L foot leads)
7. Neck slide pose 8 cts. (4 cts. on L, 4 cts. on R)
8. Shoulder shimmy pose 8 cts. (4 cts. on L, 4 cts. on R)
9. urn 8 cts. (from stage R to stage L)
10. Hip circle w/bounce 8 cts. (from R to L, in place)
11. (Reverse) Hip circle/w bounce 8 cts. (from L to R)
12. Camel walk 24 cts. (in circle, 4 cts. each; stage R L)
13. Figure 8 16 cts. (slide back/circle forward, in place)
14. Camel walk 24 cts. (in circle, 4 cts. each; stage L R)
15. Figure 8 16 cts. (slide forward/circle back, in place)
16. Turn 6 cts. (in place)/Arm circle pose w/up & down hip shimmy (or vibration) 2 cts.
17. Hip thrusts 32 cts. (in circle, stage R L; RRLR, LLRL, RRLR, LLRL, RRLR, LLRL, RRLR, LLRL)
18. Hip circle w/bounce 8 cts. (from R to L, in place)
19. (Reverse) Hip circle w/bounce 8 cts. (from L to R)
20. Hip shimmy drop pose 6 cts. (in place)
21. Walking hip shimmy 32 cts. (in square, 8 cts. each side, R foot leads)
22. Neck slide pose 8 cts. (4 cts. on R, 4 cts. on L)
23. Shoulder shimmy pose 8 cts. (4 cts. on R, 4 cts. on L)
24. Turn 8 cts. (from stage L to stage R)
25. Walking hip shimmy 32 cts. (in square, 8 cts. each side, L foot leads)

26. Neck slide pose 8 cts. (4 cts. on L, 4 cts. on R)
27. Shoulder shimmy pose 8 cts. (4 cts. on L, 4 cts. on R)
28. Turn 8 cts. (from stage R to center stage)
29. Spin 16 cts. (in place, w/skirt edges up optional; reverse direction of Turn #28 above)

Beginner Dance #2

JASMINE DANCER

Choreographed in 1994, music by Ramal Lamar, *Pleasure Gardens of Dance*

NOTE:

This dance can be performed as a solo, duet or group of 4 dancers.

The instructions are written for the dancer(s) on the Right side of stage who are leading with their right foot.

Veil Entrance Dancers on **Right**

Hold 3 cts., then do Neck Slides in place—8 x (lead w/R); Walk forward, 4 cts. half time (lead w/R)

Do Veil Swirls to R, while turning to R, 2 x; Do Veil Turn (Front) while turning to R 1.25 x; Backbend Pose (face L)

Bring veil around to front, do Veil Flutters walking back; Flip veil over the head to discard in back

Wrist Circle pose in place (from overhead to hip level)

Pose w/knees bent for next move; Begin playing finger cymbals on the drum section

Veil Entrance Dancers on **Left**

Hold 3 cts., then do Neck Slides in place—8 x (lead w/L); Walk forward, 4 cts. half time (lead w/L)

Do Veil Swirls to L, while turning to L, 2 x; Do Veil Turn (Front) while turning to L 1.25 x; Backbend Pose (face R)

Bring veil around to front, do Veil Flutters walking back; Flip veil over the head to discard in back

Wrist Circle pose in place (from overhead to hip level)

Pose w/knees bent for next move; Begin playing finger cymbals on the drum section

DANCERS ON *RIGHT* SIDE

1. Up & Down Hip Shimmy, lead w/R, 16 cts.
2. Twisting Hip Shimmy in place RLRL, 4 cts
   Shoulder Shimmy in place, RLRL, 4 cts
   Twisting Hip Shimmy in place RLRL, 4 cts
   Shoulder Shimmy in place, RLRL, 4 cts
3. Hip Thrust RR, LL, RR, 6 cts
   Neck Slide RL, 2 cts
   Hip Thrust LL, RR, LL, 6 cts
   Neck Slide LR, 2 cts
4. Camel Walk face R, 4 cts

Camel Walk face L, 4 cts
5. Twisting Hip Shimmy Walk Circle to R, 12 cts.
   Hip Circle ½, RFL, counter-clockwise, 4 cts
6. Twisting Hip Shimmy in place RLRL, 4 cts
   Shoulder Shimmy in place, RLRL, 4 cts
   Twisting Hip Shimmy in place RLRL, 4 cts
   Shoulder Shimmy in place, RLRL, 4 cts
7. Hip Thrust RR, LL, RR, 6 cts
   Neck Slide RL, 2 cts
   Hip Thrust LL, RR, LL, 6 cts
   Neck Slide LR, 2 cts
8. Camel Walk face R, 4 cts
   Camel Walk face L, 4 cts
9. Twisting Hip Shimmy Walk Circle to R 16
10. Shoulder Shimmy Rock face F, 4 cts
    Face L, 4 cts
    Face B, 4 cts
    Face R, 4 cts
11. Basic 4 Step/Karshlimar face F, 4 cts
    Face L, 4 cts
    Face B, 4 cts
    Face R, 4 cts
12. Twisting Hip Shimmy in place RLRL, 4 cts
    Shoulder Shimmy in place, RLRL, 4 cts
    Twisting Hip Shimmy in place RLRL, 4 cts
    Shoulder Shimmy in place, RLRL, 4 cts
13. Hip Thrust RR, LL, RR, 6 cts
    Neck Slide RL, 2 cts
    Hip Thrust LL, RR, LL, 6 cts
    Neck Slide LR, 2 cts
14. Camel Walk face R, 4 cts
    Camel Walk face L, 4 cts
15. Twisting Hip Shimmy Walk to L then turn L 8 cts.
    Twisting Hip Shimmy Walk to R then turn R 8 cts.
16. Turn to L, then pose! DANCERS ON *LEFT* SIDE

Beginner Dance #3

VARTER VEIL DANCE

Choreographed in 1984, music by Harry Saroyan *Saroyan Sings*

NOTE:

This dance can be performed as a solo, duet or group of 4 dancers

The instructions are for dancers beginning on the LEFT side of stage, leading with their left foot. The dancers on the Right side of the stage lead with their right foot

The dancers on the left side of stage begin the dance facing the right dancer, instead of facing front to the audience.

ENTRANCE/DANCE SECTION

1. Camel Walk 3 times to R (RLR, LRL, RLR)/Turn 4 cts in place (end up facing L);
   Camel Walk 3 times to L (RLR, LRL, RLR)/Turn 4 cts. in place, Pose 1-2 cts. facing audience
2. Camel Walk 3 times forward (RLR, LRL, RLR);
   Figure 8-2 times in place (4 cts. each);
   Hip Circle 2 times (2 cts. facing aud., 2 cts. to face R)
3. Camel Walk 4 times to R (RLR, LRL, RLR, LRL);
   Hip Circle 2 times (4 cts. facing R, 2 cts. to face aud.);
   Rib Circle 2 times in place

UNTUCK SECTION

4. Figure 8-8 cts. (1/2 circle to back);
   Figure 8-8 cts. (1/2 circle to front, while untucking front of veil);
   Neck slide pose 4 cts. (on L), Neck slide pose 4 cts. (on R);
   Turn to L 8 cts.
5. Sail Veil turn 8 cts.;
   Sail Veil overhead turn 8 cts.;
   Figure 8-16 cts. (in full circle while gathering top edge of veil)

UNTUCK/VEIL SECTION

6. Camel Walk 3 times to R (RLR, LRL, RLR)/Turn 4 cts in place (end up facing L w/veil overhead);
   Camel Walk 3 times to L (RLR, LRL, RLR)/Turn 4 cts. in place, Pose 1 2 cts. facing audience (w/veil overhead)
7. Camel Walk 3 times forward (RLR, LRL, RLR w/veil overhead);
   Figure 8-2 times in place (4 cts. each*);
   Hip Circle 2 times (2 cts. facing aud., 2 cts. to face R*)

*while bringing top veil edge in front
8. Camel Walk 4 times to R (RLR, LRL, RLR w veil face canopy);
   Hip Circle 2 times (4 cts. facing R, 2 cts. to face aud.**);
   Rib Circle 2 times in place (w/veil rib canopy)
   **w/veil held in front of body, plain

VEILWORK SECTION
9. Veil Swirls to R 8 cts.;
   Veil Turn Front to R 8 cts.;
10. Neck slide pose 4 cts. (on L), Neck slide pose 4 cts. (on R); w/veil neck canopy
    Veil Turn Front to L 8 cts.
11. Veil Swirls to L 8 cts.;
    Veil Turn Back to L 8 cts.;
    Airplane Turn or Veil Flounce pose 4 times (RLRLRLRL) 16 cts.;

DISCARD SECTION
12. Camel Walk 3 times to R (RLR, LRL, RLR)/Turn 4 cts in place (Veil Member of Aud., or gracefully discard veil to side of stage, end up facing L w/);
    Camel Walk 3 times to L (RLR, LRL, RLR)/Turn 4 cts. in place,
    Turn opposite direction 3-4 cts., end up w/pose facing aud.

VEIL SUGGESTIONS:

36" or 54" wide fabric may also be used; with length of veil to be determined by your height: a short to medium height dancer could use a 2 to 2 1/2 yd. veil, a medium height dancer could use a 2 1/2 to 2 3/4 yd. veil, a tall dancer could use a 2 3/4-3 yd. veil etc.

Beginner Dance #4

BEDOUIN WEDDING Cane Dance to Beledi

Choreographed in 1983, music by Ibrahim Farrah *Music of the Qaria*

1. *Intro*: *Soloist* can do free style or same as group dance; *Group*: Do Vibration during entire Intro. 1-Arm Circles w/cane R, T, L, B, R, then B, L, T, R, B, arch/backbend up to T; 2-Hip Figure 8 arms down T-P; 3-Rib Circle arms up B-eye level; 4-Neck Slides then cane down to chest level

   LEAD W/OUTSIDE FOOT (*Group* dancers on R use R lead foot; on L use L foot)

2. *Entrance* Hip Shimmy, Twisting—travel 20 cts. (*Soloist*—around perimeter of stage, whether square, circular, etc.; *Group* travel in square L-R, F-B, L-R, F-B, cont. F-B, 4 cts each)

   *Solo R dancer travels to L; Group travels to **inside** of square*

3. Basic karshlimar step w/hip shimmy 16 cts. (right foot leads, 4 cts. F, 4 cts. L, 4 cts. B, 4 cts. R) w/cane circles

4. Pedal turn 16 cts. (4 cts. ea. turn) w/cane twirls overhead

5. Jump/shimmy/shimmy/shimmy 16 cts. (4 cts. F, 4 cts. L, 4 cts. B, 4 cts. R) cane overhead/cane in back angled w/ R side up, cane in back, cane angled w/L side up

6. Basic beledi 4 cts. R then L side; 1-2-3 Turn 4 cts. R then L side cane follows hands

7. Shoulder shimmy rock 16 cts. (4 cts. F, 4 cts. L, 4 cts. B, 4 cts. R) cane follows hands or goes from wrist to elbow area/Change weight to L foot; stay facing R for Camel Walk

8. Camel Walk 16 cts. (4 cts. on R, 4 cts. in F, 4 cts. on L, 4 cts. in B) Soloist—R foot leads, Group outside foot leads, cane follows hands

9. Arm circles w/back to audience 6 cts. (3 cts. on L, 3 cts. on R.) cane follows hands

   *Solo R dancer travels to R; Group travels to **outside** of square*

10. Balance cane on head 16 cts. (while doing hip shimmy or vibration to distract audience)

11. Twist hips 16 cts. (4 cts. in B, 4 cts. on L, 4 cts. in F, 4 cts. on R) cane is balanced on head

12. Basic karshlimar step w/hip shimmy 28 cts. (7 x 4 cts) (4 cts. in B, 4 cts. on L, 4 cts. in F, 4 cts. on R, 4 cts. in B, 4 cts. on L, 4 cts.

in F take cane off head) while cane is balanced on head hands are continuously back then front, opposite of working hip.

13. Twist hips 16 cts. (4 cts. in F, 4 cts. on R, 4 cts. in B, 4 cts. on L) cane follows hands
14. Step 2-3 16 cts. (4 cts. in F, 4 cts. on R, 4 cts. in B, 4 cts. on L) cane does Figure 8 on same side as lead hip
15. Jump/shimmy/shimmy/shimmy 16 cts. (4 cts. in F, 4 cts. on R, 4 cts. in B, 4 cts. on L) Use same cane directions as in #5.

16. Balance cane on L shoulder 16 cts. while doing Step 2-3: 4 cts. in F, 4 cts. on R, 4 cts. in B, 4 cts. on L
17. Turn 16 cts. w/cane balanced on L shoulder (*Solo* dancer turn to R, *Group* dancers turn outside, balance cane on R shoulder)
18. Exit 6 cts.: Walking hip shimmy w/cane in hands

Key: R=Right, L=Left, B=Back or Bottom, F=Front, T=Top. *Musical phrases* #3, 6, 10, 13 male singer; #4, 7, 11, 14 chorus singers; #5, 8, 12, 15-18 instrumental

Beginner Dance #5

TOMZARA Tambourine Dance to 9/8 Karshlimar
Choreographed in 1984, music by Hatchig Kazarian *Armenia, Armenia*

NOTES:

This can be performed as a solo, duet or 4 group dancers.

Instructions are written for the front and back dancers on the RIGHT side. These dancers are on the Right side and lead with their right foot, unless they switch to the right side of the square. The front & back dancers on the Right side begin by leading with their Right foot.

The Basic KARSHLIMAR step refers to the 4 part step in front, for dancers on left this would be starting with the weight on the R foot, then step forward with the L foot, step in place with the R foot, step in back with the L foot, step in place with the R foot.

1. Hip drops in place, 2X
2. Hip drops in place, 2X, w/Tam hip hits
3. Basic Karshlimar FLBR, 1/4 circle, w/Tam hands, RIGHT FOOT LEADS
4. Basic Karshlimar, FBF, 1/2 circle
5. Basic Karshlimar, F, full circle
6. Grapevine to L, 2X (face audience)
7. Hop (FBF) in front/Shoulder Shimmy
    Hop on left/Shoulder Shimmy
    Hop in back/Shoulder Shimmy
8. Grapevine to R, 2X (back to audience)
9. Hop (FBF) in back/Shoulder Shimmy
    Hop on right/Shoulder Shimmy
    Hop in front/Shoulder Shimmy
10. Turn to R, 3 cts., w/Tam claps
    Turn to L, 3 cts., w/Tam claps
    Turn to R, 3 cts., w/Tam claps
    Arm Circle in place, 3 cts., w/Tam shake
11. Turn to L, 3 cts., w/Tam claps
    Turn to R, 3 cts., w/Tam claps
    Turn to L, 3 cts., w/Tam claps
    Arm Circle in place, 3 cts., w/Tam shake
12. Basic Karshlimar FRBL, 1/4 circle (w/Tam hands) LEFT FOOT LEADS
13. Basic Karshlimar FB, 1/2 circle
14. Basic Karshlimar F, 1 (full) circle
15. Grapevine to R, 2X (face audience)
16. Hop (FBF) in front/Shoulder Shimmy

Hop on right/Shoulder Shimmy
Hop in back/Shoulder Shimmy

17. Grapevine to L, 2X (back to audience)
18. Hop (FBF) in back/Shoulder Shimmy
    Hop on left/Shoulder Shimmy
    Hop in front/Shoulder Shimmy
19. Turn to L, 3 cts., w/Tam claps
    Turn to R, 3 cts., w/Tam claps
    Turn to R, 3 cts., w/Tam claps
    Arm Circle in place, w/Tam shake
20. Turn to R, 3 cts., w/Tam claps
    Turn to L, 3 cts., w/Tam claps
    Turn to R, 3 cts., w/Tam claps
    Arm Circle in place (w/Tam shake)
21. Jump (bend LRL) in front, w/Tam hands
    Jump (bend LRL) to left, w/Tam hands
    Jump (bend LRL) to back, w/Tam hands
    Jump (bend LRL) to right, w/Tam hands
    Jump (bend LRL) in front, w/Tam hands
22. Arm circle in place, w/Tam shake/Pose

BEGINNER DANCE EXAMINATION & CHECKLIST

Student Name: _____

Instructor Name: _____

Exam Date: _____

1. In what countries did Middle Eastern Dance originate?

   a. _____
   b. _____
   c. _____
   d. _____
   e. _____

2. Define the term "Belly Dance" _____
   _____

3. What four basic body parts can be isolated?
   a. _____
   b. _____
   c. _____
   d. _____

4. Name and illustrate six directions that most body parts can move or be isolated in:
   a. _____
   b. _____
   c. _____
   d. _____
   e. _____
   f. _____

5. What can be four basic components/parts of veil dancing:
   a. _____
   b. _____
   c. _____
   d. _____

Dance Performance Checklist, the student must perform the following dances before advancing to the Intermediate Level:

Beginning Level
3.   Raks Leyla, cabaret with finger cymbals to 4/4
4.   Jasmine Dancer, cabaret w/veil and finger cymbals
3.   Varter, veil dance
4.   Bedouin Wedding, cane dance to beledi
5.   Tomzara, tambourine dance to 9/8

Gypsy

Intermediate Dance #1

AMBERA Veil Intro w/Beledi & Ayoub Sections
Choreographed in 1986, music by Ramal Lamar, *Pleasure Gardens of Dance*

NOTE:

Solo or Group Dance: This works well for a soloist who is leading with the Right foot and starting on the Left side of the stage. But we have also performed this as a Duet and Group Dance with 4 dancers by using the Right and Lefts for duet and R front, R back, L front & L back for a group.

Starting Positions: A soloist will start this dance leading with the Right foot, from the Back Right corner, travel to front, then to left front, then to left back, then to left front. For group the soloist keeps same position, but the dancer opposite her will lead with the Left foot and start from the Back Left, travel to front, then to the right front, then to the right back and then to the right front. A group of 4 dancers will have the dancers starting from the Front Right & Left ending up in the back Left & Right, respectively.

CAPE/VEIL ENTRANCE
1. Entrance—32 cts. w/veil or cape in back, draped around shoulders, starting onstage
   Walk—6 cts. RLRLRL/Turn—2 cts. to right RL;
   Walk—6 cts. RLRLRL/Turn—2 cts. to right RL;
   Walk—6 cts. RLRLRL/Turn—2 cts. to right RL;
   Walk—6 cts. RLRLRL/Step—step pose (open veil)—2 cts. in place RL.

2. Walk—4 cts. to right RLRL/Turn—4 cts. to right in place RLRL;
   Walk—4 cts. to left LRLR/Turn—4 cts. to left in place LRLR;
   Walk—4 cts. to right back stage RLRL/Turn—4 cts. to right in place RLRL;
   Walk—4 cts. to left back stage LRLR/Turn—4 cts. to left in place LRLR.
   (Variation: Walk LRL—hold/Turn RLR—hold; repeat 3 more times)

3. Veil swirls in place toward right—4 cts./Veil "dip" in place—2 cts.;
   Veil swirls in place toward left—4 cts./Veil "dip" in place—2 cts.;
   Veil turn w/veil in back to right—4 cts./Veil "sweep" in place—2 cts.;
   Veil turn w/veil in back to left—4 cts./Veil "sweep" in place—2 cts.

4. Walk—4 cts. to right center stage RLRL/Turn—4 cts. to right in place RLRL;
   Walk—4 cts. to left center stage LRLR/Turn—4 cts. to left in place LRLR.

5. Veil swirls in place toward right—4 cts.;
    Veil turn w/veil in back to left—4 cts.;
    Walk forward toward right—4 cts. RLRL;
    Flip veil overhead then walk backwards—4 cts. RLRL;
    Walk towards center stage back and discard veil—4 cts. RLRL;
    Walk to center stage w/back to audience—4 cts. RLRL.

BEGAN ZILLS: (Beledi or 4/4 single, double or triple)

6. Hip Twist—2—3 from back to audience to facing audience 1/2 circle toward right—8 times (lead foot: RLRLRLRL). (Variation: do 2 hip twists, then 4 hip lifts in circle, then 4 hip twists.)

7. Cross-step, cross-step, cross-step, cross-step to center front—8 cts. RL LR RL LR/Side **camel** in place—4 cts.;
    Cross-step, cross-step, cross-step, cross-step to left—8 cts. RL LR RL LR /**Maya** in place—4 cts.;
    Cross-step, cross-step, cross-step, cross-step to right—8 cts. RL LR RL LR /"Pick up Baby" (**hip circle** from L to R normal, down, up) in place—4 cts./**Rib drops** in place—2 cts. w/R arm up—L arm to side pose;
    Cross-step, cross-step, cross-step, cross-step to center front—8 cts. RL LR RL LR /**Rib circle** with arm circle down/up/then down—4 cts.
    Cross-step, cross-step, cross-step, cross-step in 1/2 circle back w/ back to audience—8 cts. RL LR RL LR /**Figure 8** in place w/arm accents on first two—4 cts.;
    Cross-step, cross-step, cross-step, cross-step in full circle to back w/ back to audience—8 cts. RL LR RL LR /**Side camel** in place—8 cts.
e. Hip drop/lift in place—2 cts. (L hip w/side to audience);
    Hip drop/drop in place—2 cts. (L hip w/side to audience, then change arms);
    Rib drop/lift in place—2 cts. (same side to audience pose);
    Turn to right—4 cts. w/head "bop" up on last beat (end up facing audience with left hip up pose) RLRL;
    Hip drop/drop in place—2 cts.;
    Hip lift/lift in place—2 cts.;
    Turn to left—4 cts. LRLR.

TAXIM: No Zills

9. Free style w/standing and/or floor positions, suggestions:
    Snake arms w/floor descent (facing left side);

Knee pose w/arm circles (depending on costume/shoes);
Backbend w/snake arms or arm circles;
Arm circles or neck slide w/ascent (either side is facing audience)

ZILLS   (Ayoub rhythm, i.e. 1-2; 1 2, 1-2; 1 2, 1-2 1 2; 123)

10. Double hip lifts do 4 sets in 1/2 circle to back of stage left—6 cts. each set, RR LL RR/Hip thrusts in place—3 cts. LRL w/ hands in back; repeat above—2nd set; repeat above—3rd set; repeat above—4th set.

11. Walk—4 cts. to right forward RLRL/Turn—4 cts. to right in place RLRL Arms up pose on last beat of turn on all 4 sets;
Walk—4 cts. to left forward LRLR/Turn—4 cts. to left in place LRLR;
Walk—4 cts. to right forward RLRL/Turn—4 cts. to right in place RLRL;
Walk—4 cts. to left forward LRLR/Turn—4 cts. to left in place LRLR.

12. Hip thrusts to right—4 cts./hip thrusts in place—2 cts/turn to right 1 1/4 times;
Hip thrusts to back—4 cts./hip thrusts in place—2 cts/turn to right 1 1/4 times;
Hip thrusts to left w/back to audience—4 cts./hip thrusts in place—2 cts/turn to right 1 1/4 times;
Hip thrusts to front—4 cts./hip thrusts in place—2 cts/turn to right 1 1/4 times.

13. Double hip lifts do 2 sets in 1/2 circle to back of stage left—6 cts. each set, RR LL RR/Hip thrusts in place—3 cts. LRL w/ hands in back;

14. Figure 8 w/hip thrusts in place w/back to audience—8 cts. (R2 L2 R2, L R);
Figure 8 w/hip thrusts in 1/2 circle to face audience—8 cts. (L2 R2 L2, R L);
Figure 8 w/hip thrusts to right—6 cts. RL RL RL/Up & down shimmy in place-3 cts. RLR;
Figure 8 w/hip thrusts to left—6 cts. LR LR LR/Up & down shimmy in place—3 cts. LRL;
Figure 8 w/vibration to right—6 cts. RL RL RL/Up & down shimmy in place—
3 cts. RLR;
Figure 8 w/vibration to left—6 cts. LR LR LR/Up & down shimmy in place—
3 cts. LRL;

15. Step—2—3 (glide)—3 times RLR LRL RLR in 1/2 circle to back, end up facing audience w/arm circle pose.

16. Double hip lifts do 3 sets in 1/2 circle from back of stage to center stage—6 cts, each set RR LL RR/Hip thrusts in place—3 cts. LRL w/ hands in back;
Walk—4 cts. to center front RLRL/Turn—4 cts. to right in place RLRL; arms up pose on last beat of turn/Hip drop/lift pose—2 cts. on L hip.

17. Turn—about 3 cts. to left/Pose—1 ct.

Intermediate Dance #2

TAMZARA Group Tambourine Dance to 9/8 Karshlimar
Choreographed in 1986, music by Brothers of the Baladi, *Food of Love*

NOTES:
Instructions are written for the front and back dancers on the LEFT side. These dancers are on the Left side and lead with their left foot, unless they switch to the right side of the square. The front & back dancers on the Right side begin by leading with their Right foot.

The Basic KARSHLIMAR step refers to the 4 part step in front, for dancers on left this would be starting with the weight on the R foot, then step forward with the L foot, step in place with the R foot, step in back with the L foot, step in place with the R foot.

Phrase #1

1. Intro about 8-10 cts.: The 4 Dancers Run to center stage with tambourine "jingle" in R hand—arm at low level to above head. Note: the dancers enter from opposite corner, but end up in front right, front left, back right, back left in square formation
2. Turn-inside of square, 6 cts. or 2X, (when drum start) tambourine starts at low level then up, low level then up (end up with L hip facing audience diagonally)
3. Soft hip thrusts-6 cts. or 2X, Tam in R hand goes up 3 cts., down 3 cts.,

Phrase #2

4. Basic Karshlimar step-4 times, L foot leads in front, R side, back, L side w/hop and/or hip shimmy (Tam in R hand hits L hand at chest level)
5. Basic Karshlimar-4 times, L foot leads in front, back, front, front w/ hop and/or hip shimmy (Tam hits L hand-chest level to L side)
6. Hop-hop-hop/Shoulder shimmy to R-4 times, L foot leads w/Tam jingle-jingle-jingle/hit-hit-hit
7. Turn to L/hip U-D Tam hits R hip, turn to R/chest-chest, turn to L/hip U-D Tam hits R hip, turn to R/chest-chest (then change lead foot to R)

Phrase #3 (Repeat phrase #2, with R as lead foot & opposite directions)

8. Basic Karshlimar step-4 times, R foot leads in front, L side, back, B side (Tam in R hand hits L hand-chest level)
9. Basic Karshlimar-4X, R foot leads in front, back, front, front (Tam hits R hip in front first 3X, then goes overhead on last one)
10. Hop-hop-hop/Shoulder shimmy to L-4 times, R foot leads w/Tam jingle-jingle-jingle/hit-hit-hit

11. Turn to R/chest-chest, turn to L/hip U-D Tam hits R hip, turn to R/chest-chest, turn to L/hip U-D Tam hits R hip

Phrase #4 (a continuation of step used in #11)
12. Hip thrust to R-4 cts. Tam hits R hip 4X, turn in place 3 cts. or 1 1/4 times (face R wall)
Hip thrust to B-4 cts. Tam hits R hip 4X, turn in place 3 cts. or 1 1/4 times (back to aud.)
Hip thrust to L w/back to aud.-4 cts. Tam hits R hip 4X, turn in place 3 cts. or 1 1/4 times (face L wall)
Hip thrust to F-4 cts. Tam hits R hip, turn in place 3 cts. or 1 1/4 times (face aud.)

13. Turn in circle (from larger to smaller) 18 cts. or 3X/drop

Phrase #5
14. Floor pose with tambourine circle across front then side w/jingle-about 6 ct. or 2 measures; come up with tam jingle 1 measure or 3 cts.; turn tambourine upside down with shakes 1 measure.

Phrase #6
15. Basic Karshlimar-4 times, L foot leads in front, R side, back, L side w/Tam shakes w/hip thrust or shimmy
16. Basic Karshlimar-4 times, L foot leads in front, R side, back, L side w/Tam overhead drumming & more hip shimmies

Phrase #7
17. Basic Karshlimar to R-1 measure w/Tam shake; turn in place-1 measure w/Tam overhead drumming (L foot leads in all of #17)
Basic Karshlimar to B-1 measure w/Tam shake; turn in place-1 measure w/Tam overhead drumming
Basic Karshlimar to L, w/back to aud-1 measure w/Tam shake; turn in place-1 measure w/Tam overhead drumming
Basic Karshlimar to F-1 measure w/Tam shake; turn in place-1 measure w/Tam overhead drumming

Phrase #8 (Repeat Phrase #6 using R as lead foot, opposite directions)
18. Basic Karshlimar-4 times, R foot leads in front, L side, back, R side w/Tam shakes
19. Basic Karshlimar-4 times, R foot leads in front, L side, back, R side w/Tam overhead drumming & more hip shimmies

Phrase #8

20. Basic Karshlimar to L-1 measure; turn in place-1 measure
Basic Karshlimar to R-1 measure; turn in place-1 measure

Phrase #9

21. Karshlimar Grapevine to R in circle to back-1 measure w/Tam drumming; Karshlimar Grapevine to R in circle to back-1 measure w/Tam shaking.

Phrase #10

21. Pose with Tam circle across front to L then across front to R, then turn and end with Tam up on last beat
22. Exit hitting Tam with shimmy walk.

NOTES

1. F=front, B=back, L=right, R=back, Tam=tambourine, Aud=audience, U=up, D=down, X=times
2. One full measure equals 6 beats 1-2-3 123, 1/2 measure equal 3 beats either 1-2-3 or 123
3. This dance can also be performed Cabaret Style with finger cymbals played 1-2-3 123, or 1, 123, 123, 12, 123

Intermediate Dance #3

AMAYGUENA, Spanish Double Veil Dance
Choreographed in 1990, music by Trans Arabian Sound Band,
Moon Over Cairo III

Double Veil Entrance: Suggested-use 2 circular veils, one could be sheer (i.e. lace) and the other opaque (i.e. tissue lame). I use a Black lace veil with lace ruffle and a Red Tissue Lame veil with ruffles. Cheat: Glue or sew 2 sets of velcro dots on corresponding sides of both veils so they can be "held together" until you are ready to rip separate them.

Solo or Group Dance: This works well for a soloist who is leading with the Right foot and starting on the Right side of the stage. But we have also performed this as a Duet and Group Dance with 4 dancers by using the Right and Lefts for duet and R front, R back, L front & L back for a group.

AMAYAGUENA
1. CHORUS: With veils in "sandwich" sheer veil in front
    a. Walk-4 cts/Turn-4 cts (turn is double-time, 8-cts fast)
    b. Walk-4 cts/Turn-4 cts (turn is double-time, 8-cts fast)
    c. Walk-4 cts/Turn-8 cts (turn is double-time, 8-cts fast)

Enter from left side of stage to right side in one-half circle, end up in center stage front

2. Sub-Chorus (Right Side):
    a. Hip thrust to R-4 cts, w/sharp veil thrust on R hip
        Turn to R-4 cts.
    b. Hip thrust to R-4 cts, w/sharp veil thrust on R hip
        Turn to R-4 cts.

3. Veil flounce to frame face, 4-cts on L
    Veil flounce to frame face, 4-cts on R
4. Turn to R-4 cts.
5. Walk to Center stage front-4 cts. w/sheer veil framing face

6. Sub-Chorus (Left Side):
    a. Hip thrust to L-4 cts, w/sharp veil thrust on L hip
        Turn to L-4 cts.
    b. Hip thrust to L-4 cts, w/sharp veil thrust on L hip
        Turn to L-4 cts.

7. Veil flounce to frame face, 4-cts on R
   Veil flounce to frame face, 4-cts on L
8. Turn to L-4 cts.
9. Walk to Center stage front-4 cts. w/sheer veil framing face

10. a. Veil flounces with veils at hip level on one side and then the other-8 cts.
    b. Turn-8 cts.
    c. Veil flounces with veils at hip level on one side and then the other-8 cts.
    d. Walk towards Center Stage Back—then flip sheer veil behind you.

11. Sharp Veil Flounce/Thrusts (in 1/4 circle from back of stage to center stage front—4 times (each time take 2 steps, then flounce 2 cts.)

12. Turn with both veils behind you-8 cts.

13. Veil Swirls turning the opposite direction-8 cts.

14. CHORUS: with both veils behind you
    a. Walk-4 cts/Turn-4 cts (turn is double-time, 8-cts fast)
    b. Walk-4 cts/Turn-4 cts (turn is double-time, 8-cts fast)
    c. Walk-4 cts/Turn-8 cts (turn is double-time, 8-cts fast)

       Circle from center of stage to right side in one-half circle, end up in center stage front

15 Sub-Chorus (Right Side):
    a. Hip thrust to R-4 cts, w/sharp veil thrust on R hip
       Turn to R-4 cts.
    b. Hip thrust to R-4 cts, w/sharp veil thrust on R hip
       Turn to R-4 cts.

16. Veil flounce to frame face, 4-cts on L
    Veil flounce to frame face, 4-cts on R
17. Turn to R-4 cts.
18. Walk to Center stage front-4 cts. w/sheer veil framing face

19. Sub-Chorus (Left Side):
    a. Hip thrust to L-4 cts, w/sharp veil thrust on L hip
       Turn to L-4 cts.

b. Hip thrust to L-4 cts, w/sharp veil thrust on L hip
Turn to L-4 cts.

20. Veil flounce to frame face, 4-cts on R
Veil flounce to frame face, 4-cts on L
21. Turn to L-4 cts.
22. Walk to Center stage front-4 cts., adjust veils for "matador" turn on R arm

23. a. "Matador" turn to L—8 cts.
b. "Matador" turn to R—8 cts., then do 1/2 veil swirl to put both veils behind you

24. Turn to L—12 cts., with both veils behind you

25. Turn to R with veils separated (sheer in one hand, opaque in the other—until final note

To Get Rid of Veils:
a.) Do an arm circle and throw them behind you, out of the way at the same time (more dramatic);
b.) Or, Gather them both in left or right hand and toss them offstage (less dramatic).

NOTE:
When performing both dances back to back, you may want to consider adding about 5 to 10 "blank" spaces in between both songs on the recording for applause at the end of *Amayaguena*.

El Porompompero Latin-style Drum Solo/Finale
Choreographed in 1999, music by Hossam Ramzy,
Latin American Hits for Bellydance

NOTE:
The instructions are written for the dancer beginning on the Left side, leading with the Right foot
Can be performed as a solo, duet or 4 dancers in group

A.) Chorus: (play zills only on drum accents)
1.) Grapevine[1] to R, lead with R foot RLRL, 4 cts. (half-time slow during 7 cts.)
Turn to R in place, RL, 2 cts.
Rib Drops, bring arms down, 2 cts.

1. Grapevine[1] to diagonal L, lead with L foot LRL, 4 cts.
   Turn to L in place, LR, 2 cts.
   Rib Circle, w/arms close to face, 2 cts.
2. Grapevine[1] to diagonal R, lead with R foot, RLRL, 4 cts.
   Turn to R, in place, RL, 2 cts.
   L Hip Drops, face R, LL, 2 cts.

B. Sub-Chorus
   1. Hip Thrust front & Back LRLRLRLRLRLR, face R, 12 cts.
      Turn to L, 1 ¼ (end up facing R), 4 cts.
   2. Hip Thrust front & Back RLRLRLRLRLRL, face L, 12 cts.
      Turn to R, 1 1/2 (end up facing L), 4 cts.
   3. Hip Thrust front & Back LRLRLRLRLRLR, face R, 12 cts.
      Turn to L, 1 ¼ (end up facing F), 4 cts.

C. Melody
   1. Grapevine[2] to L, lead with R foot, 14 cts.
      Turn to R in place, 3 cts. /R Hip Thrust
   2.) Karshlimar face front, R foot leads, 3 cts.
      Karshlimar face back, R foot leads, 3 cts.
      Karshlimar face front, R foot leads, 3 cts.
      Turn to R in place, 3 cts.
   3.) R Hip Lift in circle to R, Arms do low-high, 10 cts.
      Turn to R in place, 4 cts.
   4.) Grapevine to R, lead with L foot, 14 cts.
      Turn to L in place, 3 cts. /L Hip Thrust
   5.) Karshlimar face front, L foot leads, 3 cts.
      Karshlimar face back, L foot leads, 3 cts.
      Karshlimar face front, L foot leads, 3 cts.
      Turn to L in place, 3 cts.
   6.) L Hip Lift in circle to L, Arms do low-high, 10 cts.
      Turn to L in place, 4 cts.

D. Flute Section
   1.) Step-together-step in ½ circle to R (end up in back), w/arms
      overhead sway, Feet are RLR, etc., 12 cts.
      Turn to R in place w/arm hi-low pose, 4 cts.
   2.) Step-together-step in ½ circle to R (end up in front), w/arms
      overhead sway, Feet are RLR, etc., 12 cts.
      Turn to R in place w/arm hi-low pose, 4 cts.
   3.) Step-together-step in line (end up in back), w/arms overhead
      sway, Feet are RLR, etc., 12 cts.

Turn to R in place w/arm hi-low pose, 4 cts.

4.) Step-together-step in line (end up in front), w/arms overhead sway, Feet are RLR, etc., 12 cts.

Turn to R in place w/arm hi-low pose, 4 cts.

E. Drum Solo Section

1. Hip Shimmy in place, face aud., Arms stay up overhead for Hip Shimmy, 12 cts.

Shoulder Shimmy in place, face aud., Bring arms shoulder level for Shoulder Shimmy, 4 cts.

2. Walking Hip Shimmy to back, while facing aud., bring arms up, 8 cts.

3. Walking Hip Shimmy in circle to R, bring arms down, 8 cts.

4. Walking Shoulder Shimmy to front of stage, bring arms up, feet criss cross RLRL, 8 cts.

G.) Chorus: Play zills on Grapevine step, but not on drum accents

1.) Grapevine[1] to R, lead with R foot RLRL, 4 cts. (half-time slow during 7 cts.)

Turn to R in place, RL, 2 cts.

Rib Drops, bring arms down, 2 cts.

2.) Grapevine[1] to diagonal L, lead with L foot LRL, 4 cts.

Turn to L in place, LR, 2 cts.

Rib Shimmy, w/arms close to face, 2 cts.

3.) Grapevine[1] to diagonal R, lead with R foot, RLRL, 4 cts.

Turn to R, in place, RL, 2 cts.

L Hip Drops, face R, LL, 2 cts.

H.) Sub-Chorus:

1.) Hip Thrust front & Back LRLRLRLRLRLR, face R, 12 cts.

Turn to R, 1 ¼ (end up facing L), 4 cts.

2.) Hip Thrust front & Back LRLRLRLRLRLR, face L, 12 cts.

Turn to L, 1 1/2 (end up facing R), 4 cts.

3.) Hip Thrust front & Back LRLRLRLRLRLR, face R, 12 cts.

Turn to R, 1 ¼ (end up facing F), 4 cts.

I.) Melody:

2. Grapevine[2] to L (travel in full circle), lead with R foot, 14 cts.

Turn to R in place, 3 cts./R Hip Thrust

2.) Karshlimar face front, R foot leads, 3 cts.

Karshlimar face back, R foot leads, 3 cts.

Karshlimar face front, R foot leads, 3 cts.

Turn to R in place, 3 cts.

Key

1. Grapevine[1]—R foot step forward to R, L foot step in place, R foot step backward on R, L foot step in place (reverse for L lead foot)
2. Grapevine[2]—R foot cross over L foot traveling to L, L foot step in place, R foot cross over L foot in back, L foot step in place (reverse for L lead foot)
3. *Finger Cymbals*: Can be used with the dance, 4/4 triple, but optional

Intermediate Dance #4

THE SWORD DANCE
Choreographed in 1993, music by Light Rain Band, *Dream Dancer*

Created as a Solo Dance, but can be adapted as a duet or group dance with 4 by using opposite sides of stage in the front or the back.

A.   TAXIM ENTRANCE:

1.   Enter, holding sword under straight veil)
2.   Turns w/veil edges up
3.   Discard veil w/left hand, hold sword w/right hand, (or, keep on head)
4.   Vibrations w/sword circles, back to audience
5.   Continue vibrations—balance sword on head—until "drums" start

B.   CHIFTITELLI:

1.   Maya, 2 times in place, facing front
     Maya, 2 times, facing left
     Maya, 2 times, back to audience0
     Maya, 2 times, facing right
2.   Descent w/shoulder shimmies (or other upper body undulation)
3.   Berber Walk-2 times, forward
4.   Floor turn #1-I full to left, then 1 full to right, w/arm circles
5.   Knee slides-2 times to right
6.   Snake-in-Basket (hip circle, then rib circle)-1 time, at stage right
7.   Knee slides-2 times to left
8.   Snake-in-Basket-1 time, at stage left
9.   Berber Walk-1 or 2 times, to center stage
10. Floor turn #2-1 full (to "emphasized" section of music)
11. Hinge w/vibration facing stage right
12. Hinge w/vibration facing stage left
13. Berber Walk-2 times, to back stage (put cymbals on while doing vibration)
14. Ascent w/shoulder shimmies

C.   FINALE:

1.   Maya-in circle, until end of music
2.   Pose-w/sword in hands (or, keep sword on head if you wish to continue dancing with it in drum solo or finale)

Intermediate Dance #5

KALAMATIANO, Skirt Dance to 7/8
Choreographed in 1983, music by Hatchig Kazarian, *Armenia, Armenia*

NOTE:

Solo or Group: this dance can be performed as a solo, duet or group of 4 dancers. The soloist would start on the LEFT side of the stage leading with the Right foot. For a duet, the opposite dancer would be on the Right side of the stage leading with the Left foot. For a group dance the remaining 2 dancers start on the Left back or Right back.

Section 1: with Zills

1. Hold, in place w/both arms up—6 counts
2. R Hip Thrust out-in/in, out-in/in, out-in/in, turn-2-3, R-LL, R-LL, R-LL, R-LR
   L Hip Thrust out-in/in, out-in/in, out-in/in, turn-2-3, L-RR, L-RR, L-RR, L-RL
   R Hip Thrust out-in/in, out-in/in, out-in/in, turn-2-3, R-LL, R-LL, R-LL, R-LR
   L Hip Thrust out-in/in, out-in/in, out-in/in, turn-2-3, L-RR, L-RR, L-RR, L-RL
   R Hip Twist-2-3, L Hip Twist-2-3, R Hip Twist-2-3, Turn-2-3 (F-BF, F-BF, F-BF, L-RL) to L
3. R Hip Twist-2-3, L Hip Twist-2-3, R Hip Twist-2-3, Turn-2-3 (F-BF, F-BF, F-BF, L-RL) to B
   R Hip Twist-2-3, L Hip Twist-2-3, R Hip Twist-2-3, Turn-2-3 (F-BF, F-BF, F-BF, L-RL) to F
   R Hip Twist-2-3, L Hip Twist-2-3, R Hip Twist-2-3, Turn-2-3 (F-BF, F-BF, F-BF, L-RL) to F
   L Hip Thrust out-in/in, out-in/in, out-in/in, turn-2-3, L-RR, L-RR, L-RR, L-RL
4. R Hip Thrust out-in/in, out-in/in, out-in/in, turn-2-3, R-LL, R-LL, R-LL, R-LR
   L Hip Thrust out-in/in, out-in/in, out-in/in, turn-2-3, L-RR, L-RR, L-RR, L-RL
   R Hip Thrust out-in/in, out-in/in, out-in/in, turn-2-3, R-LL, R-LL, R-LL, R-LR
5. R Hip Drop-2-3, L Hip Drop-2-3, R Hip Drop-2-3, Camel-2-3, Step L-RR, R-LL, L-RR, RLR

R Hip Drop-2-3, L Hip Drop-2-3, R Hip Drop-2-3, Camel-2-3,
Step L-RR, R-LL, L-RR, RLR
(Dancers A & B do this while traveling to back row, facing the
audience), while at the same time,
Dancers C & D do the steps below while traveling to the front
row—C & D are inside square)
A and C continue to lead with the *Right*, while B and D continue
to lead with the *Left*:
R Hip Lift-2-3, L Hip Lift-2-3, R Hip Lift-2-3, Camel-2-3,
Step L-RR, R-LL, L-RR, RLR
R Hip Lift-2-3, L Hip Lift-2-3, R Hip Lift-2-3, Camel-2-3,
Step L-RR, R-LL, L-RR, RLR

6. R Hip Twist-2-3, L Hip Twist-2-3, R Hip Twist-2-3, Turn-2-3
    (F-BF, F-BF, F-BF, L-RL) to L
    R Hip Twist-2-3, L Hip Twist-2-3, R Hip Twist-2-3, Turn-2-3
    (F-BF, F-BF, F-BF, L-RL) to F
    R Hip Twist-2-3, L Hip Twist-2-3, R Hip Twist-2-3, Turn-2-3
    (F-BF, F-BF, F-BF, L-RL) to R
    R Hip Twist-2-3, L Hip Twist-2-3, R Hip Twist-2-3, Turn-2-3
    (F-BF, F-BF, F-BF, L-RL) to B

7. R Hip Push-step/step face *IN*, L Hip Push-step/step face **OUT**
    (R-LR, L-RL)
    R Hip Thrust-2-3 face **OUT**, L Hip Thrust-2-3 face **OUT**
    R Hip Push-step/step face **OUT**, L Hip Push-step/step face *IN*
    (R-LR, L-RL)
    R Hip Thrust-2-3 face *IN*, L Hip Thrust-2-3 face *IN*

Section 2: without Zills

8. R Hip Push-step/step face *IN*, L Hip Push-step/step face **OUT**
    (R-LR, L-RL)
    R Hip Thrust-2-3 face **OUT**, L Hip Thrust-2-3 face **OUT**
    R Hip Push-step/step face **OUT**, L Hip Push-step/step face *IN*
    (R-LR, L-RL)
    R Hip Thrust-2-3 face *IN*, L Hip Thrust-2-3 face *IN*

9. Skirt Flounce w/o Zills: Step-2-3, Step-2-3, Step-2-3, Turn-2-3,
    R-LR, L-RL, R-LR, L-RL

    a.) Face *In*/Out/In/Turn to *Front* (Dancers A & B), C & D In/
        Out/In/Turn to Back
    b.) Face *Front*/Back/Front/Turn to *Out* (Dancers A & B), C &
        D Back/Front/Back/Out

c.) Face *Out*/In/Out/Turn to *Back* (Dancers A & B), C & D Out/In/Out/Turn to Front

d.) Face *Back*/Front/Back/Turn to *In* (Dancers A & B), C & D Front/Back/Front/In

e.) Face *In*/Out/In/Turn to *Front* (Dancers A & B), C & D In/Out/In/Turn to Back

f.) Face *Front*/Back/Front/Turn to *Front* (Dancers A & B), C & D Back/Front/Back/Front

Note that the last turn in front is a double turn and all dancers end up facing the audience

Section 3: with Zills

10. R Hip Thrust out-in/in, out-in/in, out-in/in, turn-2-3, R-LL, R-LL, R-LL, R-LR
L Hip Thrust out-in/in, out-in/in, out-in/in, turn-2-3, L-RR, L-RR, L-RR, L-RL/POSE

Finger Cymbal Suggestions:

1. Basic: 1-23, 1-23, 1-23, 1-23 (or R-LR, L-RL, R-LR, L-RL)
2. Embellishment #1: 1-123, 1-2, 1-2; 1-123, 1-2, 1-2; 1-123, 1-2, 1-2; (R-LRL, RL, RL)
3. Embellishment #2: 1-123, 1-123, 1-2; 1-123, 1-123, 1-2 (R-LRL, R-LRL, RL)

Costume Suggestions:

Turkish, Gypsy or Romany style ruffled skirt w/sleeved blouse, vest, harem pants and coined bra, belt & jewelry.

INTERMEDIATE DANCE EXAMINATION & CHECKLIST

Student Name: _____

Instructor Name: _____

Exam Date: _____

1. What are step variations: _____

    _____

    Give an example: _____

    _____

2. What are step combinations: _____

    _____

    Give an example: _____

    _____

3. What are step transitions: _____

    _____

4. Name 3 different ways to play finger cymbals:

    a. _____
    b. _____
    c. _____

5. Name 2 other words for finger cymbals:

    a. _____
    b. _____

Dance Performance Checklist, the student must perform the following dances before advancing to the Advanced Level:

Intermediate Level

1. Ambera, cabaret w/cape entrance
2. Tamzara, group tambourine dance to 9/8
3. Amayaguena/El Porompompero, Spanish double veil w/drum solo finale
4. The Sword Dance
5. Kalamatiano, skirt dance to 7/8

Opa Azel

Advanced Dance #1

BAHIA, Egyptian-style Cabaret solo
Choreographed in 1989, music by The Best of YaSalaam, *Bahia*

1. Intro, 8 cts., w/zills, offstage
2. Walk-walk/hip-hip, 16 cts (1st aisle?)
   WWHH, WWHH, WWHH, WWHH, unless otherwise noted, right
   hip always leads, i.e.: RLRR LLRL RRLR LLRL
3. Turn, 8 cts. to R (change zills, muted or tingle for example)
4. Repeat #2 above (2nd aisle?)
5. Turn, 4 cts
6. a-Basic karshlimar, 12 cts. (R foot leads, go to L) b-Hip thrust in 1/2
   circle-4 cts. (R hip leads, go to R)
7. a-Repeat #6a (L foot leads, go to R) b-Repeat #6b (L hip leads, go to L)
8. Hip-hip/walk-walk, 16 cts (1st aisle?)
   HHWW, HHWW, HHWW, HHWW, unless otherwise noted, right
   hip always leads, i.e.: RLRR LLRL RRLR LLRL
9. Turn, 8 cts. to R (change zills, muted or tingle for example)
10. Repeat #8 above (2nd aisle?)
11. Turn, 4 cts
12. a-Basic karshlimar, 12 cts. (R foot leads, go to L) b-Hip thrust in 1/2
    circle-4 cts. (R hip leads, go to R)
13. a-Repeat #12a (L foot leads, go to R) b-Repeat #12b (L hip leads, go to L)
14. Double hip lifts, 16 cts. (in self circle)
15. a-Basic beledi, 8 cts. (R, then L side) b-Turn-2-3, 8 cts. (R, then L
    side) c-Camel walk, 8 cts. (to face back)
16. a-Basic beledi, 8 cts. (R, then L side); w/back to aud. b-Turn-2-3, 8 cts.
    (R, then L side); w/back to aud. c-Camel walk, 8 cts. (to face aud.)
17. a-Tush push w/vibration to R, 6 cts. b-Tush push w/vibration to L, 4
    cts. c-R hip-drop forward/drop back/drop forward/drop sharp, upper
    body tuck (face L)-4 cts. d-Shoulder shimmy pose (down then up),
    ummy ummy into rib undulation then sharp drop-2 cts.
18. Reda step, 6 cts./turn, 2 cts., face front
    Reda step, 6 cts./turn, 2 cts., face right
    Reda step, 6 cts./turn, 2 cts., face back
    Reda step, 6 cts./turn, 2 cts., face left
19. a-Basic beledi, 8 cts. (R, then L side) b-Turn-2-3, 8 cts. (R, then L
    side) c-Camel walk, 8 cts. (to face back)
20. a-Basic beledi, 8 cts. (R, then L side); w/back to aud. b-Turn-2-3, 8 cts.
    (R, then L side); w/back to aud. c-Camel walk, 8 cts. (to face aud.)

21. a-Tush push w/vibration to R, 6 cts. b-Tush push w/vibration to L, 4 cts. c-R hip-drop forward/drop back/drop forward/drop sharp, upper body tuck (face L)-4 cts. d-Shoulder shimmy pose (down then up), ummy ummy into rib undulation then sharp drop-2 cts.
22. Turn-2-3, slow to R, 3 cts., R arm pose down then up,
    Turn-2-3, slow to L, 3 cts., L arm pose down then up,
    Turn-2-3, fast to R, 3 cts., Shoulder shimmy down then up,
    Turn-2-3, fast to L, 3 cts., Shoulder shimmy down then up,
23. a-Grapevine, 12 cts. to R in circle, L foot leads b-Turn, 4 cts to L (LRL, hold weight on R) c-Grapevine, 12 cts. to R in circle, L foot leads d-Turn, 4 cts to L (LRL, hold weight on R) e-Grapevine, 8 cts. to R in circle, L foot leads f-Turn, to L g-Hip circle w/vibration in place
24. Hip-step, 24 cts. in self circle (R arm up then down . . . both arms up), lead with R foot
25. a-Cha Cha step, 8 cts, instead of basic Beledi RL RLR LR LRL b-Turn-2-3, 8 cts. (in self circle) c-Camel walk, 16 cts., (R foot leads, L foot leads, R foot leads, L foot leads)
26. Turn, 8 cts.
27. Walking hip shimmy, 16 cts.
28. Turn, 8 cts.
29. Double hip lifts, 16 cts.
30. Turn, 20-22 cts., w/zill accents/POSE!!!

Advanced Dance #2

ZANNUBE, 4-part Egyptian Cabaret Dance, 10:00 Min.
Choreographed in 1985, music by, The Sultans, *The Best of the Sultans*;
The Sultans *Saidi Wind*

ZANUBBE: Zills to 4/4 Beledi

1   Taxim Entrance: Enter w/veil draped around back, do a few veil turns, "flirt" or "play" w/audience as you go to center stage back, discard veil, do a few undulations w/back to audience while you wait for drumming to begin.

2   Drum Intro: Hip Thrust_8 cts. (RR, LL, RR, LR in place)

3   Reda Step_16 cts. (an "Up & Down" Hip shimmy, foot goes up w/same side hip: LRLRLRLRLRLRLRLR, in circle, hands "paddle" up & down to accent hip work, begin zill work

4   CHORUS: Double Hip Lifts_16 cts. (forward, R foot leads);
Reda Step_8 cts. (in circle, RLRLRLRL);
Double Hip Drops_4 times (backwards, L foot leads);
Turn_8 cts. (towards your right, R foot leads)

5   CHORUS: Double Hip Drops_16 cts. (backward, L foot leads);
Reda Step_8 cts. (in circle, LRLRLRLR);
Double Hip Lifts_4 times (forwards, R foot leads);
Turn_8 cts. (towards your left, L foot leads)

6   SUB CHORUS: Karshlimar Step_16 cts. (in circle, FLBR, R foot leads)

7   ACCENT #1: Hip Thrusts_6 times (towards your right, R foot leads, R hip & foot go front then back);
Turn_3 cts. (RLR);
Hip Thrusts_6 times (towards your left, L foot leads, L Hip & foot go front then back);
Turn_3 cts. (LRL)

8   ACCENT #2: Rib drops_8 cts. (2 cts. each on LRLR, weight is on R foot, L foot, R foot, then L foot, stepping back facing audience diagonally)

9   CHORUS: Double Hip Lifts_16 cts. (forward, R foot leads);
Reda Step_8 cts. (in circle, RLRLRLRL);
Double Hip Drops_4 times (backwards, L foot leads);
Turn_8 cts. (towards your right, R foot leads)

10   SUB CHORUS: Karshlimar Step_16 cts. (in circle, LBRL, L foot leads)

11   ACCENT #1: Hip Thrusts_6 times (towards your left, L foot leads, L Hip & foot go front then back);
Turn_3 cts. (LRL);
Hip Thrusts_6 times (towards your right, R foot leads, R hip & foot go front then back);
Turn_3 cts. (RLR);

12   ACCENT #2: Rib drops_8 cts. (2 cts. each on LRLR, weight is on R foot, L foot, R foot, then L foot, stepping back facing audience diagonally)

13   CHORUS: Double Hip Lifts_16 cts. (forward, R foot leads);
Reda Step_8 cts. (in circle, RLRLRLRL);
Double Hip Drops_4 times (backwards, L foot leads);
Turn_8 cts. (towards your right, R foot leads)

14. CHORUS: Double Hip Drops_16 cts. (backward, L foot leads);
Reda Step_8 cts. (in circle, LRLRLRLR);
Double Hip Lifts_4 times (forwards, R foot leads);
Turn_4 cts. (towards your left, L foot leads)

15. Turn_20 cts. (in place or in circle going towards your R, R foot leads)/Head Snap (Lift) on last accent beat

NEY TAXIM: Slow rhythm with or without Zills
1.   Arm Circles facing front
Arm Circles facing left side w/floor pose, then up
Arm Circles facing front
Arm Circles facing right side w/floor pose, then up
Arm Circles facing front, make transition into Rib Circle

2.   Rib Circle facing front
Rib Circle facing left side
Rib Circle facing front
Rib Circle facing right side
Rib Circle facing front

3.   Maya facing front (Hips lower RL, RLR)
Maya facing left side (LR, LRL)
Maya facing back (RL, RLR)
Maya facing right side (LR, LRL)

4.   Maya facing diagonally back towards your right (RLR)
Maya facing diagonally back towards your left (LRL)
Maya facing diagonally back towards your right (RLR)
Maya facing diagonally back towards your left (LRL)

5.   Camel Walk going forward, facing diagonal left (RLR)
Camel Walk going forward, facing diagonal right (LRL)

Camel Walk going forward, facing diagonal left (RLR)
Camel Walk going forward, facing diagonal right (LRL)

6. Camel Walk going backward, facing diagonal left (LRL)
Camel Walk going backward, facing diagonal right (RLR)
Camel Walk going backward, facing diagonal left (LRL)
Camel Walk going backward, facing diagonal right (RLR)

7. Side Camel facing front (Hips rise RL, RLR)
Side Camel facing left (LR, LRL)
Side Camel facing back (RL, RLR)
Side Camel facing right (LR, LRL)

8. Figure Eight_2 complete 8's (slide forward, circle back)
9. Rib Circle_2 complete circles (FLBR, FLBR)/ Shoulder
Shimmy/Rib Drop

DRUM SOLO: (Zills to various drum rhythms)

1. MUSMOODY

Hip Thrusts_4 cts to L/Hi Thrusts_4 cts in place (LLRL) Hip Thrusts_4
cts to B/Hip Thrusts_4 cts in place (LLRL) Hip Thrusts_4 cts to
R/Hip Thrusts_4 cts in place (LLRL) Hip Thrusts_4 cts to F/Hip
Thrusts_4 cts in place (LLRL);
Grapevine Step w/Shoulder Shimmy_12 cts. (crossover w/L foot, step
back w/R foot_3 in F, 3 in B, 3 in F, 3 in B);

Hip Thrusts_4 cts to R/Hip Thrusts_4 cts in place (RRLR)
Hip Thrusts_4 cts to B/Hip Thrusts_4 cts in place (RRLR)
Hip Thrusts_4 cts to L/Hip Thrusts_4 cts in place (RRLR)
Hip Thrusts_4 cts to F/Hip Thrusts_4 cts in place (RRLR);

2 HEAVY/ACCENTED BEAT:
Rib drop drop/swing swing_32 cts. (in circle, 4 cts. each combination_8 times)

3 2/4:
Karshlimar Step_16 cts. (in diamond, L foot leads, FRBL);
Hip Thrust_16 cts. (in diamond, L foot leads, FRBL, L hip
& foot goes front then back);
Karshlimar Step_16 cts. (in diamond, R foot leads, FLBR);
Hip Thrust_16 cts. (in diamond, R foot leads, FLBR, R hip

& foot goes front then back);

4   BELEDI:
    Basic Beledi_2 times (R then L side, R then L foot leads)
    Turn_3 cts. (R then L side, RLR then LRL)/Rib Drop
    Basic Beledi_2 times (R then L side, R then L foot leads)
    Turn_3 cts. (R then L side, RLR then LRL)/Rib Drop

5   4/4:
    Shoulder Shimmy_6 cts. (facing R side, diagonally)/Rib
    Lift/Drop/Lift accent;
    Shoulder Shimmy_6 cts. (facing L side, diagonally)/Rib
    Lift/Drop/Lift accent;
    Shoulder Shimmy_6 cts. (facing R side, diagonally)/Rib
    Lift/Drop/Lift accent;
    Shoulder Shimmy_6 cts. (facing L side, diagonally)/Rib
    Lift/Drop/Lift accent;

6   DRUMS:
    Camel Walk forward_3 cts. (R foot leads, face L,)
    Camel Walk forward_3 cts. (L foot leads, face R,)
    Camel Walk forward_3 cts. (R foot leads, face L,)
    Camel Walk forward_3 cts. (L foot leads, face R,)
    Camel Walk forward_3 cts. (R foot leads, face L,);
    Turn back to audience

7   DRUM ROLL:
    Hip Shimmy (up & down, or Vibration) w/"Figure 8" arms_ w/back
    to audience;
    Turn w/"Airplane" arms';
    Hip Shimmy (up & down, or Vibration) w/"Figure 8" arms_ facing
    audience)/Rib Drop on last "accent" beat

8   Hip Thrusts_16 cts. (RRLR, LLRL, RRLR, LLRL, face FRBL)

9   Turn_9 cts./Head Snap (lift) on last "accent" beat

FINALE:

1   Hip drops in place_8 cts.

2   1_2_3 Step (Glide)_6 times (in 1/2 circle to back, R foot leads, go
    towards stage right);
    Turn_3 cts. (in place, RLR-hold);

1_2_3 Step (Glide)_6 times (in 1/2 circle to front, L foot leads, go towards stage left);
Turn_3 cts. (in place, LRL-hold);

3   Karshlimar Step_3 times, 4 cts. each (in place, front center stage FLB, R foot leads);
Turn_3 cts. (in place, RLR);
Karshlimar Step_3 times, 4 cts. each (in place, front, center stage FRB, L foot leads);
Turn_3 cts. (in place LRL);

4.   Walk_12 cts. (1/2 circle towards your left, R foot leads)
Turn_3 cts. (in place RLR);
Walk_12 cts. (1/2 circle to stage right, L foot leads)
Turn_3 cts. (in place LRL)

5.   Hip Thrust_3 times, 4 cts. each (in place, center stage FLB, R foot leads, hip & foot go front then back);
Turn_3 cts. (in place (RLR);
Hip Thrust_3 times, 4 cts. each (in place, center stage FLB, L foot leads, hip & foot go front then back);
Turn_3 cts. (in place (LRL);

6.   1_2_3 Step (Glide)_6 times (in 1/2 circle to back, R foot leads, go towards stage right);
Turn_3 cts. (in place, RLR-hold);
1_2_3 Step (Glide)_6 times (in 1/2 circle to front, L foot leads, go towards stage left);
Turn_3 cts. (in place, LRL-hold);

7.   Karshlimar Step_3 times, 4 cts. each (in place, front center stage FLB, R foot leads);
Turn_3 cts. (in place, RLR);
Karshlimar Step_3 times, 4 cts. each (in place, front, center stage FRB, L foot leads);
Turn_3 cts. (in place LRL);

8.   Walk_16 cts. (complete circle, start towards L side, R foot leads)
Turn_9 cts. (in place or circle)/Head Snap (Lift) on last "accent" beat

Advanced Dance #3

Welcome To The Dance, Cabaret style with Beledi, 9/8 and Musmoody
Choreographed by in 1985, music by Steve Flynn *Welcome to the Dance*

Hold, 16 cts. (play zills after 8 cts., can use Beledi w/embellishment)

1. Set #1 (accent every 8 cts.)
    a.) Walking Hip Shimmy (with Sunset arm circles, in circle to R), 24 cts.
    b.) Turn to R, 8 cts.

2. Set #2 (6 sets LRRR, RLLL, LRRR, RLLL, LRRR, RLLL, in circle to L)
    a.) Cross-step/Hip Drop-Drop, 24 cts.
    b.) Turn to L, 8 cts.

3. ACCENT #1
    a.) Shoulder Shimmy pose on R, look over R shoulder, back to aud., 8 cts.
    b.) Shoulder Shimmy pose on L, look over L shoulder, back to aud., (then turn to R)
    d.) Shoulder Shimmy pose on F, face aud., 8 cts.

4. Set #3 (to Left in circle)
    a.) Double Hip Lifts (lead with R hip), 24 cts.
    b.) Turn to R, 8 cts.

5. ACCENT #2
    a.) Left Hip Drop pose, look over L shoulder w/back to aud., 8 cts.
    b.) Right Hip Drop pose, look over R shoulder w/back to aud., 8 cts. then turn to L
    c.) Left Hip Drop pose, facing aud., 8 cts.

6. Set #4 (same as Set #1, accent every 8 cts., except go in circle to Left)
    a.) Walking Hip Shimmy (with arm circles), 24 cts.
    b.) Turn to L, 8 cts.

7. Music section change
    a.) Travel Hip Thrust to L, lead w/L foot, (w/L foot front & back), face aud., 12 cts.
         Turn 4 cts. to L
    b.) Travel Hip Thrust to R, lead w/L foot, (w/L foot front & back), back to aud., 12 cts.

Turn 4 cts. to L
- c.) Grapevine to R, lead w/R foot, back to aud., 12 cts.
  Turn 4 cts. to R
- d.) Grapevine to R, lead w/R foot, face aud., 12 cts.
  Turn 4 cts. to R

8. ACCENTS
   - a.) Tush Push to R, 3 times, hold
     Turn to Left, hip thrust
     Turn to Right, hip thrust
   - b.) Tush Push to R, 3 times, hold
     Turn to Left, hip thrust
     Turn to Right, hip thrust

9. Beledi (Left foot leads)
   - a.) Karshlimar face F, then turn, 8 cts.
   - b.) Karshlimar face L, then turn, 8 cts.
   - c.) Karshlimar face B, then turn, 8 cts.
   - d.) Karshlimar face R, then turn 8, cts.

10. Present Sways (1/2 Sunset, inside to out); facing Left side
    - a.) L Arm Sway
    - b.) R Arm Sway
    - c.) Both Arms Sway
    - d.) L hip drop
    - e.) R hip drop

    Repeat Present Sways facing Right side

    - a.) R Arm Sway
    - b.) L Arm Sway
    - c.) Both Arms Sway
    - d.) R hip drop
    - e.) Shoulder shimmy, w/Rib drop at end, facing aud.

11. Beledi (Right foot leads)
    - a.) Karshlimar face F, then turn, 8 cts.
    - b.) Karshlimar face R, then turn, 8 cts.
    - c.) Karshlimar face B, then turn, 8 cts.
    - d.) Turn to Right in circle, 16 cts

12. Set #5
    a.) Walking Hip Shimmy, in circle to R, 24 cts.
    b.) Turn to R, 8 cts.

13. Set #6 (6 sets LRRR, RLLL, LRRR, RLLL, LRRR, RLLL, in circle to L)
    a.) Cross-step/Hip Drop-Drop, 24 cts.
    b.) Turn to L, 8 cts.

14. ACCENT #3
    a.) Shoulder Shimmy pose on R, look over R shoulder, back to aud., 8 cts.
    b.) Shoulder Shimmy pose on L, look over L shoulder, back to aud., (then turn to R)
    d.) Shoulder Shimmy pose on F, face aud., 8 cts.

Set #7 (accent every 8 cts.)
a.) Double Hip Lifts (lead with L or R hip), in circle to R, 24 cts.
b.) Turn to R, 8 cts.

YASALAAM Drum Solo
Choreographed in 1996, music by YaSalaam, *Volume 3*

Intro, I ct. (Dance starts w/o Zills)

1.) 3/4 Up & Down Hip Shimmy, R foot leads, travel to front of stage, arms down to up, 12 cts.
Figure 8 w/Hip Thrust in place on R L R L, 4 cts.
3/4 Up & Down Hip Shimmy, R foot leads, travel to back (face aud), arms come in, then do 1/2
Sunset Circle, 12 cts.

2.) Attitude Walk in circle to L, R foot leads, arms shoulder level, 16 cts.

R Arm Point/Hip Thrust to Front, then 1/2 spin to face back (towards L), 4 cts.
R Arm Point/Hip Thrust to Back, then 1/2 spin to face front (towards L), 4 cts.
Turn w/Hip Up & Down Shimmy in Circle to Left, R foot leads, 8 cts.

R Arm Point/Hip Thrust to Right Side, then 1/2 spin to face Left (towards L), back to aud., 4 cts.

R Arm Point/Hip Thrust to Left Side, then 1/2 spin to face front (towards L), 4 cts.

4.) R Hip Lift, travel to R, Lift 2 3; Drop Lift, 8 cts.
L Hip Lift, travel to L, Lift 2 3; Drop Lift, 8 cts.

5.) L Hip Thrust Front Back, face Front, Feet LRLR, Look Front Back, 5 cts.
L Hip Thrust Front Back, face Right, Feet LRLR, Look Front Back, 5 cts.
L Hip Thrust Front Back, face Back, Feet LRLR, Look Front Back, 5 cts.
L Hip Thrust Front Back, face Left, Feet LRLR, Look Front Back, 5 cts.

6.) Forward Undulation, Rib Circle (Counterclockwise), Ummy Ummy, Rib Drop Drop w/Cat Arms; facing R Diagonal; (3 cts. x 4 moves), 12 cts.
Forward Undulation w/Rib Shimmy, Rib Circle (Counterclockwise) w/Rib Shimmy, Ummy Ummy,
Rib Drop Drop w/Cat Arms; facing L Diagonal; (3 cts. x 4 moves), 12 cts.

R Arm Lunge down on side, w/Hip Thrust on R, I ct.
L Arm Lunge down on side, w/Hip Thrust on L, I ct.

Walk in 1/2 oval to R until back to aud., 3 cts.
Look over L shoulder 2 cts.
Cont. Walk in 1/2 oval to R, until facing aud., 3 cts.
Rib Drop Lift in place, 2 cts.

9.) R Hip Reda Shimmy in 1/2 circle to R until back to aud., 20 cts.

10.) Tush Push w/Vibration in a circle to R, L foot leads (start and end w/ back to aud.), 16 cts.

Vibration w/back to aud., Arms to Figure 8 on L side, R side, L side; look over L R L shoulder, then turn R

Cont. Vibration facing aud., Arms to Figure 8 on R side, L side; look R L
Cont. Vibration w/ Arms down to up, accent Ribs then Hips

Shoulder Shimmy to Floor, pose then up

Zill Section
11.) Zar Turn to L in circle, 24 cts.

12.) Reda Shimmy w/arms from down to up, face Front, 8 cts.
Reda Shimmy w/arms from down to up, face Right, 8 cts.
Reda Shimmy w/arms from down to up, face Back, 8 cts.
Reda Shimmy w/arms from down to up, face Left, 8 cts.

13.) Shoulder Shimmy Walk to R, R foot leads, 6 cts.
Head Flip, down up, 2 cts.
Shoulder Shimmy Walk to L, L foot leads, 6 cts.
Head Flip, down up, 2 cts.

14,) L Hip Drop, travel in circle to L, 24 cts.

15.) Walk, until back to aud., 16 cts.

16.) Shoulder Shimmy Turn to L, 8 cts.

Shoulder Shimmy in place, face aud., 8 cts.

Shoulder Shimmy Down/Up, 4 cts.

Bow

Welcome To The Dance, Cabaret Finale
Choreographed by in 1985, music by Steve Flynn *Welcome to the Dance*

Hold, 3 cts.

1.) Set #1
   a.) Turn to R, 12 cts.
   b.) Shoulder Shimmy Pose on R, 4 cts.

2.) Set, #2
   a.) Turn to L, 12 cts.
   b.) Shoulder Shimmy Pose on L, 4 cs.

3.) Set #3
   a.) Double Hip Lifts, travel LRLRLR hips w/arms up, 12 cts.
   b.) Turn to R, 4 cts.

4.) Set #4
    a.) Turn to L, 1 ct. Arms Down
    b.) Turn to L, 2 cts. Arms Mid-Down
    c.) Turn to L, 2 cts. Arms Mid
    d.) Turn to L, 4 cts. Arms Mid-Up
    e.) Turn to L, 5, 6, 7 Arms Up

5.) Collapse, facing front, quickly down then up, 2 cts.

6.) Turn to R

Advanced Dance #4

USKUDAR, Turkish Cabaret w/Double Veil Entrance & Zills
Choreographed in 1994, music by The Evergreen Group, *Mediterraneo*

Taxim Entrance: Have Red & Gold veils (Solo w/L Arm up, R Arm shoulder level) in both arms in front of body; run out & do *turn* to R, then
Airplane turn to R; *separate* veils and do *turn* to R, then *airplane* turn to R. *Discard* both veils before fast section of song begins. Soloist can **turn R**; Group turns to **outside**

VOCAL: Section A (Solo L foot leads, Group Inside)
1. Hip Shimmy Walk in square (soloist - circle) to L 32 cts.
2. Travel Hip Thrusts to L 12 cts.
    Turn to L 4 cts.
3. Travel Hip Thrusts to R 12 cts.
    Turn to R 4 cts.
4. Double Hip Thrusts, travel back, LRLRLRLR 12 cts.
    Turn to R 4 cts.
5. Double Hip Thrusts, travel forward, RLRLRLRL 12 cts.
    Turn to L (3/4 end up facing R side); change weight 4 cts.

INSTRUMENTAL: Section B (Solo R foot leads, Group Inside)
6. Hip Shimmy Walk in "U" (soloist - circle) to R 32 cts.
7. Arm Sweep w/Hip Thrust, on R L R L (Arms: R, L, Both, Both) 16 cts.

VOCAL
8   Travel Hip Thrusts to R 12 cts.
    Turn to R 4 cts.
9. Travel Hip Thrusts to L 12 cts.
    Turn to L 4 cts.
10. Double Hip Thrusts, travel back, RLRLRLRL 12 cts.
    Turn to L 4 cts.
11. Double Hip Thrusts, travel forward, LRLRLRLR 12 cts.
    Turn to R (3/4 end up facing L side), change weight 4 cts.

INSTRUMENTAL: Section C (Solo L foot leads)
12. Shoulder Shimmy Walk in ¾ square and then to Back to L 32 cts.
13. Arm Lunge Pose on L R L R (Arms: L, R, L Front, R Front) 16 cts.

VOCAL

14. Travel Hip Thrusts to L (Group face F or B dancer; soloist w/Back to Audience) 12 cts.
    Turn to L 4 cts.
15. Travel Hip Thrusts to R, (Group face F or B dancer; soloist w/Back to Audience) 12 cts.
    Turn to R 4 cts.
16. 3/4 Hip Twist, travel back, LRLRLRLRLRLR (travel halfway across) 12 cts.
    Turn to L 4 cts.
17. 3/4 Hip Twist, travel forward, RLRLRLRLRLRL (travel the other half across) 12 cts.
    Turn to R 4 cts.

INSTRUMENTAL: Section D (Solo R foot leads)

18. Shoulder Shimmy travel forward to front, step half time 12 cts.
    R Hip Thrust, pivot turn to R 4 cts.
    Shoulder Shimmy travel to back w/back to aud., step half time 12 cts.
    L Hip Thrust, pivot turn to L 4 cts.
19. Travel Neck Slide to R (w/Dahlal Arm Pose), Group to inside 12 cts.
    Turn to R, cont. neck slide 4 cts.
    Travel Neck Slide to L (w/Dahlal Arm Pose), Group to outside 12 cts.
    Turn to L, cont. neck slide 4 cts.

VOCAL

19. Travel Hip Thrusts to R 12 cts.
    Turn to R 4 cts.
20. Travel Hip Thrusts to L 12 cts.
    Turn to L 4 cts.
21. Double Hip Lifts travel forward (or back), RRLLRRLL 12 cts.
    Step forward LRLR (bring both arms up, Sunrise) 4 cts.
22. R Hip Thrust, pivot to R 4 cts.
22. Turn to R (solo L Arm up/R Arm at shoulder level, group turns inside)

Key:

1. Group Dance Floor Patterns. Lead dancer starts Section A on Front Right; Section B on Front Left; Section C on Back R; Section D on Back L. The Dancer on Front Left uses all reverse directions of the Lead Dancer; as do the dancers in the back row. The directions are written for Lead Dancer on Front Right and can be used for a solo dance.
2. Cymbals: 1, 1-2-3-4, 1-2, 1-2 for the most part; optional use triple 123 during turns or accents

Advanced Dance #5

RO-HE, Winged Cape Entrance Dance
Choreographed in 1997, music by Hossam Ramzy, *Ro-He*

Entrance w/Cape: Walk RLR-LR, LRL-RL, RLR-LR, LRL-RL, 32 cts.

1.) To Right
   a. Turn, 8 cts.
   b. Airplane, 8 cts.
   c. Turn, 8 cts.
   d. Airplane, 8 cts.

2.) Arm Pose (back to Aud.)
   a. R Arm up, 2 cts.
   b. L Arm up, 2 cts.
   c. Both Arms close down, 2 cts.
   d. Both Arms open up, 2 cts.

3.) To Left
   a. Turn, 8 cts.
   b. Both Arms sway down, in place, 8 cts.
   c. Turn, 8 cts.
   d. Both Arms sway down, in place, 8 cts.

4.) Arm Pose (face Aud.)
   a. L Arm up, 2 cts.
   b. R Arm up, 2 cts.
   c. Both Arms close down, 2 cts.
   d. Both Arms open up, 2 cts.

5.) To Left
   a. Turn w/both arms low, 8 cts.
   b. Turn w/both arms up, 16 cts.

6.) Put Cape in front, walk around stage in circle to R, do flounce, using shoulder roll, 16 cts.

7.) To Right
   a. Turn, 8 cts.
   b. Airplane, 8 cts.
   c. Turn, 8 cts.

    d. Airplane, 8 cts.
        Both Arms Sway, 2 cts.
        Both Arms Sway, 2 cts.
        Both Arms Sway, 2 cts.
        Both Arms Sway, 2 cts.

8.) To Left
    e. Turn, 8 cts.
    f. Airplane, 8 cts.
    g. Turn, 8 cts.
    h. Airplane, 8 cts.
        Both Arms Sway, 2 cts.
        Both Arms Sway, 2 cts.
        Both Arms Sway, 2 cts.
        Both Arms Sway, 2 cts.

9.) To Right
    a. Turn w/both arms low, 8 cts.
    b. Turn w/both arms up, 16 cts.

10.) Remove cape (put in left hand, then discard)

BALADI THRILLER, Stage Dance
Choreographed in 2002, music by Samy Faraq, *Arabian Dance Fever*

1.) *Musmoody Entrance*:
    a.) Hold w/o zills 2 cts.
        L Hip Thrust face aud., 1 cts
  a. R Hip Thrust back to aud., 2 cts
        L Hip Thrust face aud., 1 cts
  b. R Hip Thrust back to aud., 2 cts
        L Hip Thrust face aud., 1 cts
  c. R Hip Thrust back to aud., 2 cts
        L Hip Thrust w/hip shimmy, face aud., 1 cts

2.) Rib Thrust R-L, weight on R foot, face aud., 2 cts
    Body wave arms up to down w/snake arms, pivot to face B,
    Rib Thrust L-R, weight on L foot, facing B, 2 cts.
    Body wave arms down then snake arms w/hip shimmy

3.) Karshlimar w/R foot, face B, R, F, 12 cts.
    Neck Slide R-L, weight on R foot, face aud., 2 cts

Body wave R arm up, L arm out w/snake arms

4.) Hip Thrust travel to L, w/L foot, face F, 6 cts.
L Arm Lunge to left in place, 2 cts.
Walking hip shimmy travel in circle to L w/L foot lead, 8 cts.
L Hip Beledi, 4 cts.

5.) Rib Thrust L-R, weight on L foot, face aud., 2 cts
Body wave arms up to down w/snake arms, pivot to face B,
Rib Thrust R-L, weight on R foot, facing B, 2 cts.
Body wave arms down then snake arms w/hip shimmy

6.) Karshlimar w/L foot, face B, L, F, 12 cts.
Neck Slide L-R, weight on L foot, face aud., 2 cts
Body wave L arm up, R arm out w/snake arms

7.) Hip Thrust travel to R, w/R foot, face F, 6 cts.
R Arm Lunge to right in place, 2 cts.
Walking hip shimmy travel in circle to R w/R foot lead, 8 cts.
R Hip Beledi, 4 cts.

8.) Step-together-step, L foot lead, travel to L w/Shoulder Shimmy, arms open then closed, 16 cts.

9.) Walk to back stage facing aud., R foot lead, end w/body wave up shoulder level, head lift, arms do figure 8 shape (Sunset down to shoulder level from overhead; then Sunset down from shoulder level to hip), 7 cts.

10.) Diagonal R Hip Thrust/Turn, travel to R front from back left, arms open then closed, 4X = 16 cts
Walk to back stage facing aud., L foot lead, end w/body wave up shoulder level, head lift, arms do figure 8 shape (Sunset down to shoulder level from overhead; then Sunset down from shoulder level to hip), 7 cts.

11.) Diagonal L Hip Thrust/Turn, travel to L front from back right, arms open then closed, 4X = 16 cts
Walk to back stage facing aud., R foot lead, end w/body wave up shoulder level, head lift, arms do figure 8 shape (Sunset down to shoulder level from overhead; then Sunset down from shoulder level to hip), 7 cts.

12.) Walk to center stage front facing aud., R foot lead, 4 cts./Turn to R
in place, 3 cts.

ZILL SUGGESTIONS—Musmoody Entrance to *Baladi Thriller*:

a.) Hold-2, 123, 1, 12345; 1-2, 123, 1, 12345 etc. for # 1 (without zill
embellishments)

b.) 1-2, 123, 1-2, 1-2, 1; 1-2, 123, 123, 123, 123 ??? for # 2, 5

c.) 1-2, 123-1, 123, 1-2 (beledi w/embellishment) for # 4, 7

d.) 123, 123, etc. for # 3, 6, 9, 12

e.) 1234567, hold; 1234567, hold; etc. for # 8

f.) 1-2, 123, 123; 1-2, 123, 123; etc. for # 10, 11 thrust/turn; then triple
123, 123 for walk

DRUM SOLO
Choreographed in 2001, music by Raks Balady, Balady Trommel

1.) Drum Trommel
   a.) L hip drop, travel forward, 6 cts. (skip first beat); Rib drop, 2 cts.
   b.) L hip drop, travel to L, 6 cts.; Rib drop, 2 cts.
   c.) Rib undulate w/shoulder shimmy, travel to B facing L, 6 cts; L
   Hip drop, 2 cts.
   d.) Rib undulate w/shoulder shimmy, travel to R facing B, 6 cts; L
   Hip drop, 2 cts.

2.) Vibration/Pose
   a.) Vibration Pose w/Figure 8, face F (arms up in center, down on
   side, repeat)
   b.) Choo Choo shimmy turn to L, 1 ½ times est., end w/back to aud.
   c.) Vibration in place w/back to aud, end w/arms up

3.) Thrust Section, 16 cts.: starts w/back to aud.
   a.) L Hip Thrust w/L Arm Thrust, cross R foot, face B;
   R Hip Thrust w/R Arm Thrust, cross L foot, face B;
   L Hip Thrust w/L Arm Thrust, cross R foot, face B hip out; face
   B hip in; face F hip out
   b.) Rib Shimmy walk in ½ circle to R, end w/back to aud., 16 cts.
   c.) R Hip Thrust w/R Arm Thrust, cross L foot, face B;
   L Hip Thrust w/L Arm Thrust, cross R foot, face B;
   R Hip Thrust w/R Arm Thrust, cross L foot, face B hip out; face
   B hip in; face F hip out

d.) Rib Shimmy walk in full circle to L, end facing aud., 16 cts.

4.) Walk/Point Section:
    a.) Walk to front w/shoulder shimmy, lead w/L foot, then point R hand to aud., 8 cts.
    b.) Walk to back w/shoulder shimmy, lead w/ L foot, then point R hand back to aud., 8 cts.

5.) Vibration/Pose Section:
    a.) Vibration pose face R, brings arms up inside Sunset, end w/ head lift, 4 cts.
    b.) Vibration pose face L, bring arms up inside Sunset, end w/ head lift, 4 cts.
    c.) Vibration pose w/figure 8 face F, bring arms up inside Sunset down down on side; shoulder shimmy

BALADI THRILLER, Finale
Choreographed in 2002, music by Samy Faraq, *Arabian Dance Fever*

1.) Walk to back stage facing aud., 8 cts.
Hip shimmy in place; head side to side, 8 cts.

2.) Hip shimmy travel in ½ circle to R, end up center front, R foot leads, 16 cts.
Turn in place to R, 8 cts.

3.) Hip shimmy travel in ½ circle to R, end up center back, R foot leads, 16 cts.
Turn in place to R, 8 cts.

4.) Hip shimmy travel forward, end up center front, R foot leads, 16 cts.
Turn in place to R, 8 cts.

5.) Hip shimmy travel back w/back to aud., end up center back, R foot leads, 8 cts.
Pivot to face aud., hip shimmy travel forward facing aud., end up center, R foot leads, 8 cts.
Shimmy/turn in place to R (slower to catch breath), 8 cts.

6.) Travel turn in circle to center front, 16 cts.

ZILL SUGGESTIONS—*Finale*:

a.)   Hold 4 cts., then 123, etc. for # 1

b.)   1-2-3-4-5-6, 123, 123, 123, 123, 123, 123 for # 2-5

c.)   123, etc. for # 6

ADVANCED DANCE EXAMINATION & CHECKLIST

Student Name: _____

Instructor Name: _____

Exam Date: _____

1. Name 3 types of Rib Movements:

    a. _____
    b. _____
    c. _____

2. Name 6 types of hip movements that have the word "hip" in it

    a. _____
    b. _____
    c. _____
    d. _____
    e. _____
    f. _____

3. Name 2 variations for hip figure 8:

    a. _____
    b. _____

4. Name 3 travel directions for hip drops or lifts:

    a. _____
    b. _____
    c. _____

5. Name two floor dance movements:

    a. _____
    b. _____

Dance Performance Checklist, the student must perform the following dances before advancing to the Group/Troupe Level:

Advanced Level
1. Bahia
2. Zannube, 4-Part Cabaret
3. Welcome to the Dance, YaSalaam Drum Solo, Finale
4. Uskudar, Turkish cabaret w/finger cymbals
5. Ro-He cape entrance, Baladi Thriller, Drum Solo, Finale

Group/Troupe Dance #1

HANNA DRUMZILZIA, Group dance with Zills to 4/4 Drums
Choreographed in 1980, music by Eddie Kochak, Volume 5

Entrance Section: (Start in line formation, posed offstage in Totem Pole
   pose (dance in front has arms out/down; dancer in center has arms
   out/shoulder level; dancer in back has arms out/up)
   Intro, 4 cts.

1.   WALKING HIP SHIMMY_20 CTS. (Enter the stage, the group does
     the twisting hip shimmy from "line" formation into "row" formation)
2.   DOUBLE HIP LIFTS_4 SETS (8 CTS. each set);
     a.   1ST SET: Dancers on R & L travel to front of stage w/hip lifts;
          while the dancer in the center travels to the back of stage w/hip
          lifts; HIPS: RR LL RR, R-drop/lift
     b.   2ND SET: All dancers do double hip lifts in place (this means
          the dancer in center is still in back; and the dancers on the
          sides are still front); HIPS: LL RR LL L-drop/lift
     c.   3RD SET: This is exactly the same as the 2nd set; repeat the
          2nd set; HIPS: RR LL RR, R-drop/lift
     d.   4TH SET: Dancers on R & L travel back to middle of stage
          w/hip lifts; while the dancer in the center travels forward to
          middle of stage w/hip lifts; HIPS: LL RR LL L-drop/lift

3.   L HIP LIFT CIRCLE_8 CTS., Hips: lift-2-3-4-5-6-L drop/lift
4.   REVERSE L HIP LIFT CIRCLE_8 CTS., Hips: lift-2-3-4-5-6-L drop/lift
5.   L HIP THRUSTS_3 SETS (8 CTS. EA.) Hips: Thrust-2-3-4-5-6-L
     drop/lift; all 3 dancers travel in oval shape circle, the dancer on the
     L end of stage leads
6.   TUSH PUSH_8 CTS. TO R; Feet: L-R, L-R, L-R, turn to face the other
     way/swing arms in half circle to frame other direction/change weight
7.   TUSH PUSH_8 CTS. TO L; Feet: R-L, R-L, R-L, use last 2 cts. to
     pose weight

Solo Section: (Start this section by posing immediately after tush push,
   dancer in center has arms up/even; dancers on right & left have one
   arm up, one arm down to frame center dancer)
8.   Left DANCER_8 CTS. (SOLO); come forward toward aud., then
     back by 8 cts.
9.   Center DANCER_8 CTS. (SOLO); same as above
10. Right DANCER_8 CTS. (SOLO); same as above

11. WALKING HIP SHIMMY_8 CTS. All Dancers (FROM FACING AUD., TO BACK TO AUD.)

Flirt with Audience Section: Peek-a-Boo

12. HIP DROPS_4 CTS. ON L, 4 CTS. ON R (Hips: drop-2-3/change sides)
13. SHOULDER SHIMMY_2 CTS. ON L, 2 CTS. ON R (look at aud. on each side)
14. HIP (Twist) SHIMMY W/BACK TO AUD._4 CTS., in place
15. REPEAT HIP DROPS
16. REPEAT SHOULDER SHIMMY
17. WALKING (Twist) HIP SHIMMY_4 CTS. (Travel from BACK TO AUD., TO FACING AUD.)

Finale Section: (after the 1:45 min. song ends; record a few cts. of silence for applause, the add the first 24 counts at the beginning of song to the tail-end of tape as "exit" music)

18. TURN_8 CTS., to R
20. TURN_8 CTS. (REVERSE) to L
21. SHOULDER SHIMMY WALK INTO "TOTEM POLE" FORMATION—8 CTS. (R foot can lead. Dancer in front bends down for floor pose, dancer in center bends so that she is in middle—the audience should be able to see all 3 dancers, dancer in back poses standing up; arms are the same as the totem pole pose used in the beginning—except the dancer in front may want to cross her arms across her chest, rather than having them out & down)

This is the 24 cts. of "Exit" music

22. Dancer in front gets up, then dances offstage to 8 cts.
23. Dancer in center dances offstage to 8 cts.
24. Dancer in back dances offstage to 8 cts.

Finger Cymbal pattern suggestions: 1, 1-2-3-4-5, 1, 1-2-3-4-5, 1, 1-2-3-4-5, 1-2; repeat and/or use Triple time 123, 123, 123, etc.

Group/Troupe Dance #2

A Whole New World, Group Veil for 4-5 dancers
Choreographed in 1993, music by Alan Menken, lyrics by Tim Rice,
Aladdin Soundtrack

INTRO: The 4 Group Dancers are posed onstage near the back, 2 on L, 2 on R (Dancers # 2 & 3 have straight veils, # 1 & 4 can use circular veils); Let one measure of music go by, about 4 6 counts, veils are in back

1. ENTRANCE: Instrumental section
    a. Dancer #1 runs onstage, toward the aud., then poses on R front, 18 cts.
    b. Dancer #2 runs onstage, toward the aud., then poses on L front, 12 cts.
    c. Dancer #3 runs onstage, toward the aud., then poses on R back, 12 cts.
    d. Dancer #4 runs onstage, toward the aud., then poses on L back, 8-10 cts.

2. VEIL FLIPS: Vocal section
    a. Dancers # I & 2 do veil flip in front, then in back, (*Aladdin*) *I can show you the world, Shining, shimmering, splendid*
    b. Dancers # 3 & 4 do veil flip in front, then in back, *Tell me, princess, now when did, You last let your heart decide?*
    c. Dancers # 1, 2, 3 & 4 do veil flip in front, then in back, *I can open your eyes, Take you wonder by wonder*

3. VEIL TURNS:
    a. Dancers # 2 & 3 do turn w/veil in back, L hands together, *Over, sideways and under, On a magic carpet ride*
    b. Dancers # I & 4 do turn w/veil in back, L hands together, *A whole new world, a new fantastic point of view*
    c. Dancers # 1, 2, 3 & 4 do turn w/veil in back, L hands together, *No one to tell us no, Or where to go, Or say we're only dreaming*

4. VEIL MAYPOLE:
    a. Dancers 1, 2, 3 & 4 join both hand, w/veils in back, then walk about 8 cts. to the Right in circle, facing inside, (*Jasmine*) *A whole new world, A dazzling place I never knew*
    b. Look at each other, facing inside the circle, and do a veil swirl at the same time, *But when I'm way up here, It's crystal clear*
    c. Look at each other, then do a backbend pose, with R hand down, L hand in back, *That now I'm in a whole new world with you*

d. Turn to face outside of circle, w/veils in back, join hands, and walk about 8 cts. to the L, Vocal end w/4 f

e. Run away from the pole, w/veils in back, return to original position and do veil swirls;, Vocal end w/4 f

f. Dancers # 1 & 4 discard veils, after doing veil swirl, Vocal end w/4 f

5. VEIL TOSS & TURN: *Unbelievable sights through Let me share this whole new world with you*

   a. Dancer #2 dances to Dancer #1 w/veil framing face, they do veil toss

   b. Dancer #3 goes under veil toss to Dancer #4 w/veil framing face, they do veil toss

   c. Dancers #1, 2, 3 & 4 do veil toss

   d. Dancers #1 & 2 do veil turn

   e. Dancers #3 & 4 do veil turn

   f. Dancers #1, 2, 3 & 4 do veil turn

6. ALL DANCERS CONTINUE VEIL TOSS SOLOIST DANCER ENTERS (During Instrumental)

   a. Dancers 1—4 do veil toss while Dancer #5 runs under veil, does veil swirls, and other standing veil movements then goes into a graceful floor

   a. Dancer 5 continues doing veil movements at floor level.

   b. Dancers 1—4 grab their individual veils gracefully and then begin doing veil swirls in the same direction. If dancer 5 is doing a veil swirl, they should match her direction.

   c. Dancers # 1, 2, 3 & 4 frame Dancers 5 on floor, pose in semi circle, hands joined with veils in back.

   d. To exit the dancer on the Left leads all 4 dancers out and "pick up" dancer # 5 on the way out.

Suggestions for a Great Veil Dance:

1. Always dance to and from different poses/positions,
2. Practice synchronized veil swirls. by looking at each other, use eye contact,
3. Do a rib circle while waiting your turn to dance. or while watching other dancers.
4. Never rush! It makes your movements look JERKY and STRAINED!
5. *Recommended Viewing*, the 1993 Oscar Awards featuring choreography by Debbie Allen and dancing by Atlantis, Veena & Neena (BellyTwins) performing to *A Whole New World*!

Group/Troupe Dance #3

PHAEDRA PHARONICA, Group Candle Dance for 4 dancers
Choreographed in 1993, music by Eddie Kochak, Volume 6

Intro: Hold 8 cts.

Section #1:
1. 2 Dancers on L side, 2 dancers on L side, walk in ½ circle to center stage, hold candles in front, close to body, 16 ct.
   Pose in line formation
2. Do Camel Walks in place, 2 times, 8 cts. (RLRL, LRLR)
3. 2 on R face R, 2 on L face 14 hold R hand up, L hand down
4. Do Rib Circles facing front, 8 cts. total

Section #2:
1. Do Camel Walks, traveling, 4 times, 16 cts. (RLRI, LRLR, RLRL, LRLR); until group is in row formation; hold candles in front, close to body
2. Stagger hand positions, then slowly switch to opposite, 2 cts. each position
   a. Dancer #1, candles down (she is in front of row)
   b. Dancer #2, candles half down (she is behind dancer #1)
   c. Dancer #3, candles half up (she is behind dancer #2)
   d. Dancer #4, candles up (she is last in row)

3. Do Rib Circles, traveling, back into line formation, 8 cts.

Section #3: Solo section (each dancer gets 16 ct. solo)
1. Dancer # 1 Hip Figure R
   a. 4 cts. travel to front, 8 cts. figure 8, 4 cts. travel back into line
2. Dancer #2 Rib Undulation
   b. 4 cts. travel to front, 8 cts. rib undulate, 4 cts. travel back into line
3. Dancer #3 Maya (vertical figure 8)
   c. 4 cts. travel to front, 8 cts. maya, 4 cts. travel back into line
4. Dancer #4 Hip Circle in a circle
   d. 4 cts. travel to front, 8 cts. hip circle, 4 cts. travel back into line

Section #4:
1. All dancers walk in circle around stage, 16 cts.; hold candles in front, close to body
   a. Then, pose in line formation

2. Do Camel Walks in place, 2 times, 8 cts. (RLRL, LRLR)
   b. 2 on Outside face Outside, 2 on Inside fare Inside; hold R hand up, L hand down
3. Do Rib Circles facing front, 8 cts. total

Section #5:
1. Do Camel Walks, traveling, 4 times, 16 cts. (RLRI, LRLR, RLRL, LRLR); until group is in row
2. formation; hold candles in front, close to body
3. Stagger hand positions, then slowly switch to opposite, 2 cts. each position
   a. Dancer #1, R hand up (she is in front of row)
   b. Dancer #2, L hand down (she is behind dancer #1)
   c. Dancer #3, R hand up (she is behind dancer #2)
   d. Dancer #4, L hand down (she is last in row)
4. Do Neck Circles, in place, 5 cts.
5. End in Totem Pole pose (Dancer #1 is down, dancer #2 is half down, dancer #3 is half up, dancer #4 is up)

Group/Troupe Dance #4

I REMEMBER EGYPT, Group Sword for 4 dancers
Choreographed in 1993, music *I Remember Egypt*

1. INTRO—8 cts. (drums, hold offstage)
2. ENTRANCE: (Line up in a square formation, one-by-one); hold sword med./chest level while running in; then sharply pose w/sword up on last count; do outside hip drops in place while waiting for other dancers to enter
   a. Dancer #1 runs onstage to front R—7 cts.
   b. Dancer #2 runs onstage to front L—7 cts.
   c. Dancer #3 runs onstage to back R—7 cts.
   d. Dancer #4 runs onstage to back L—6 cts.

3. ZAGHAREETS: (Dancers on R & L sides, do sword circles opposite)
   a. Hip thrust out w/sword ½ circles: overhead to outside—3 cts.
   b. Hip thrust in w/sword ½ circles: under to inside—3 cts.
   c. Hip thrust out w/sword ½ circles: overhead to outside—3 cts.
   d. Hip thrust in w/sword ½ circles: under to inside—3 cts.

4. SAME BEAT, BUT WITH GROUP VOCALS: Camel Walk in Your Own Circle, opposite of #4
   a. All dancers hold swords up, camel walk to inside—3 cts.
   b. All dancers hold swords down, camel walk to back—3 cts.
   c. All dancers hold swords up, camel walk to outside—3 cts.
   d. All dancers hold swords down, camel walk to front—3 cts.

5. SAME BEAT, BUT W/O GROUP VOCALS (Drums only): Same as #5, face aud.
   a. Hip thrust in w/sword ½ circles: under to inside—3 cts.
   b. Hip thrust out w/sword ½ circles: overhead to outside—3 cts.

6. SAME BEAT, BUT WITH GROUP VOCALS: Camel Walk in Your Own Circle, opposite of #4
   a. All dancers hold swords up, camel walk to inside—3 cts.
   b. All dancers hold swords down, camel walk to back—3 cts.
   c. All dancers hold swords up, camel walk to outside—3 cts.
   d. All dancers hold swords down, camel walk to front—3 cts.

7. SAME BEAT, BUT W/O VOCALS: (Drums only): Same as #5, face aud.
   a. Dancers #3 &4 do Hip Thrust out w/sword ½ circles: overhead to outside—3 cts.
      At the same time, Dancer #2 gives her sword to Dancer #1; then Dancers # 2, 3 & 4 shimmy walk to back stage, far away from swords—then pose in line formation.

8. SAME BEAT, BUT WITH SOLO VOCAL:
   a. Dancer # 1 does double swords solo—for 3 cts x 5 drum sets w/ pause; count slow.
      (Steps will include sword swirls, one in R/one in L hand, sword turns, end doing eye frame with both swords in front—for 4 sets; pose on the 5th set w/swords crossed)
      At the same time, Dancers #2 & 4 are still back of stage doing hip drops; while Dancer #3 has 15 cts. To balance sword on her head.
   b. I believe there is an extra 3 cts. drum set after the 5, we can use this for the transition into the totem pole formation.

9. SAME BEAT, BUT W/O VOCALS (Drums only):
   a. Dancer #1 gives sword back to Dancer #3, then they hip shimmy walk into next formation—3 cts.

10. SLOWER DRUMS:
   a. By now all of the dancers should be lined up in Totem Pole formation (Order: Front is Dancer #2, 1, 3, 4)
      Dancers #1, 3 & 4 do neck slides with sword framing eyes, Dancer #3 does rib circle—7 cts.
   b. Dancers #1, 3 & 4 do neck slides with sword framing eyes, Dancer #3 does rib circle—7 cts.

11. SAME SLOW DRUMS—BUT NEW INSTRUMENT COMES IN—FADE OUT ENDING:
   a. All Dancers shimmy walk to line formation, do sword ½ circle from bottom to top—7 cts.
   b. Pose—then Bow for Applause (at the same time)!

Group/Troupe Dance #5

YAHLEWA, Canes, Tambourines & Zill to Beledi for 3 dancers
Choreographed in 1982, music by Jalaleddin Takesh, *Volume 4*

A. **Slow Entrance**: Canes & Zills (All 3 enter stage, the dancer w/zills is in center)
1. Intro-8 cts.
2. Camel Walk-20 times forward ("line" formation into "row" formation)
3. Camel Walk-4 times (facing front)
4. Basic Beledi-2 times (right then left)
5. Turn-2-3/Hip Drop-2 times (right then left)
6. Basic Beledi-2 times (right then left)
7. Turn-2-3/Hip Drop-2 times (right then left)
8. Shoulder Shimmy Rock-8 times (leaning front & back)
9. Camel Walk-8 times (line goes 1/2 circle to back row, left dancer leads)
10. Camel Walk-4 times (facing front)

B. **Cane Duet Section**:
11. Hip tuck-tuck-jump-switch-8 times forward (Right & left dancers start in opposite directions, facing "fronts", then facing "backs")
12. Grapevine-8 cts. (to opposite side)
13. Grapevine-8 cts. (back to original side)
14. Jump/shimmy/shimmy/shimmy-4 times (facing: front, side, back, side-right & left dancers are opposite)
15. Cane twirls-4 times (w/cane overhead, right & left dancers are opposite)
16. Hip shimmy walk-16 cts. (One dancer balances cane on head while other dancer puts cane edges between their stomach areas)
17. Hip shimmy circle-30 cts. (with one cane between dancers and other cane on one dancer's head balanced-both dancers could use the last 2-4 seconds of this phrase to put canes back in hands and to get ready for next step)
18. Hip tuck-tuck-jump-switch-8 times backward (same as above) reverse direction
19. Camel walk-4 times (perhaps in a self-circle, to position dancers for next step)

C. **Medium Section**: Canes & Zills (The dancer in center joins in)
20. Basic beledi-2 times (right then left)

21. Turn-2-3-hip drop-2 times (right then left)
22. Basic beledi-2 times (right then left)
23. Turn-2-3-hip drop-2 times (right then left)
24. Shoulder shimmy rock-8 times (lean front & back)
25. Turn-8 cts. (Cane dancers should put canes aside and pick up tambourines for next section)

D. **Fast Section**: Tambourines & Zills
26. Intro-8 cts.
27. Basic beledi-8 cts. (left dancer only)
28. " " (left & lead dancers only)
29. " " (left, lead & right dancers)
30. " " (all dancers)
31. Shoulder shimmy rock-8 cts. (lean front & back-all)

32. Turn-2-3-hip drop (left dancer only)
33. " " (left & lead dancers only)
34. " " (left, lead & right dancers)
35. " " (all dancers)
36. Shoulder shimmy rock-8 cts. (lean front & back-all)

37. **Solo**-lead dancer w/Finger Cymbals (72 counts)

38. Turn-8 cts. to R (all)

E. **Finale Section**: Tambourines & Zills
39. Solo/bow-16 cts. (left dancer)
40. Solo/bow-16 cts. (right dancer)
41. Shoulder shimmy rock-8 cts. (lean front & back-all)
42. Turn-8 cts. (all, then pose)

NOTES:
1. FINGER CYMBAL SUGGESTIONS FOR BELEDI:
   a. 1-2, 1 = R-L, R
   b. -2, 1-2-3, 1 = R-L, R-L-R, L
   c. -2, 1-2-3, 1, 1-2-3 = R-L, R-L-R, L, R-L-R
   d. -2, 1-2-3, 1, 1-2-3, 1-2; = R-L, R-L-R, L, R-L-R, L-R;

2. TAMBOURINE SUGGESTIONS FOR BELEDI
   a. 1 2, 1
   b. 1-2, 1-2, 1

GROUP/TROUP DANCE EXAMINATION & CHECKLIST

Student Name: _____

Instructor Name: _____

Exam Date: _____

1. When dancing in group formation with 4 dancers, describe 2 different formations to arrange the group in:
   a. _____
   b. _____

2. Can all solo dances be adapted to use for a group or troupe dance?
   a. Yes _____
   b. No _____
   c. If no, then why _____
   _____

3. Besides a group cane dance, name 6 other props that a dance troupe can use when performing a group dance:
   a. _____
   b. _____
   c. _____
   d. _____
   e. _____
   f. _____

4. Is it a rule that all dance group members should perform the same exact steps at the same exact time in a group choreography?
   a. Yes _____
   b. No _____
   c. f yes, then why _____
   _____

5. Name 2 of your favorite American Belly Dance Troupes and at least 1 International Belly Dance Troupe:
   a. _____
   b. _____
   c. _____

Dance Performance Checklist, the student must perform the following dances before advancing to the Performer Level:

Group Level
1. Hanna Drumzilzia, drum solo w/finger cymbals
2. A Whole New World, group veil dance
3. Phaedra Pharonica, pharonic candle dance
4. I Remember Egypt, sword dance
5. Yahlewa, Canes, Tambourine & Zills

PERFORMER DANCES

African Queen

Performer Dance #1

DANCE RAMZA/DANCE SELMA/DANCE NAZIRA,
Cabaret Dance for Soloist or 4 dancers
Choreographed 2009, music by Eddie Kochak, *Volume 5*

DANCE RAMZA, Dance to 4/4 with Zills
Dance starts onstage, lead with Inside Foot
(on L side lead w/R foot, on R side lead w/L foot)
Soloist can choose which side to lead from then use inside L or R foot

Lead w/Inside Hip: Dancers on R side lead w/L hip, Dancers on L side lead w/R hip

1. Intro Hip Drops in place 16 cts. (8 cts. w/o finger cymbals, 8 cts. w/ finger cymbals)
   OPTIONAL: Hip Drops 8 cts. w/o cymbals, Hip Vibration 8 cts w/cymbals
2. Walking hip shimmy 32 cts. (in square, Inside, F/B, Outside, F/B, 8 cts. on each side)
3. Neck slide pose w/Temple Arms, 8 cts. (4 cts. Inside, 4 cts, Outside)
4. Shoulder shimmy pose w/Arms Out, 8 cts. (4 cts. Inside, 4 cts. Outside)
5. Travel Turn 8 cts. (if on L, turn to R; if on R, turn to L), CHANGE WEIGHT
6. Walking hip shimmy 32 cts. (in square, Inside, F/B, Outside, F/B, 8 cts. on each side)
7. Neck slide pose w/Temple Arms, 8 cts. (4 cts. Inside, 4 cts. Outside)
8. Shoulder shimmy pose w/Arms Out, 8 cts. (4 cts. Inside, 4 cts. Outside)
9. Travel Turn 8 cts. (if on L, turn to R; if on R, turn to L), CHANGE WEIGHT
   OPTIONAL: Soloist or Duet can use Circle Floor Pattern instead of Square Floor Pattern

Lead w/Outside Hip: Dancers on R side lead w/R hip, Dancers on L side lead w/L hip

10. Karshlimar (RLRL or LRLR) face F, In, Back, Out, 4 counts each side, 16 Cts.
11. Grapevine Travel to Inside, RLRL X4 or LRLR X4, 16 Cts.; THEN CHANGE WEIGHT

Lead w/Inside Hip: Dancers on R side lead w/L hip, Dancers on L side lead w/R hip

12. Karshlimar (RLRL or LRLR) face F, In, Back, Out, 4 counts each side, 16 Cts.

13. Grapevine Travel to Inside, RLRL X4 or LRLR X4, 16 Cts.; THEN CHANGE WEIGHT

Lead w/Outside Hip: Dancers on R side lead w/R hip, Dancers on L side lead w/L hip

14. FRONT ROW: Double Hip Lifts travel back, 8 Cts., then Double Hip Lifts in outside circle, 8 Cts.
    BACK ROW: Double Hip Lifts travel forward, 8 cts., then Double Hip Lifts in outside circle, 8 Cts.
15. FRONT ROW: Double Hip Lifts travel forward, 8 Cts., then Double Hip Lifts in outside circle, 8 Cts.
    BACK ROW: Double Hip Lifts travel back, 8 cts., then Double Hip Lifts in outside circle, 8 Cts.
    OPTIONAL—CHANGE WEIGHT Lead w/Inside Foot: Single Hip Lifts in inside Circle, (Arms: both down on working hip Inside Sunrise, Outside Sunset), 8 Cts.

Lead w/Inside Hip: Dancers on R side lead w/L hip, Dancers on L side lead w/R hip

16. Walking hip shimmy 32 cts. (in square, 8 cts. each side, R foot leads)
17. Neck slide pose w/Temple Arms, 8 cts. (4 cts. on R, 4 cts. on L)
18. Shoulder shimmy pose w/Arms Out, 8 cts. (4 cts. on R, 4 cts. on L)
19. Spin 16 cts. (in place, w/skirt edges up optional; reverse direction of Turn #28 above)
    OPTIONAL: Soloist or Duet can use Circle Floor Pattern instead of Square Floor Pattern

WORKING WITH FLOOR PATTERNS—*SQUARES* (or **Circles**) for Group:

1. Dancers on Right side of square pass in front when going side to side
2. Dancers on L side pass in back of Dancers on R side when going side to side
3. Dancers in Back Row travel inside the square when going front to back

4. Dancers in Front Row travel outside of the square when going front to back

FINGER CYMBAL PATTERN SUGGESTIONS:
12345678 (single time)
12345678910111213141516 (double time)
1234567891011121314151617181920212223 24 (triple time)

DANCE SELMA
Veil Dance to Rhumba
(straight veil recommended, Basic Veil Drape from Chapter 4)
Soloist will start this dance on the
Right side of stage with veil tucked on Left Arm
Group dancers on R side tuck veil on L Arm,
dancers on L side tuck veil on R Arm

Lead w/Outside Foot: Dancers on R side lead w/R foot, Dancers on L side lead w/L foot

1. Wrist Circles in place to frame Outside working hip, Veil is **tucked** w/flounces on F&B of outside Hip, 8 cts.
2. Front Camel Walk, Face F, In, Back, Out, Turn Out (i.e. R-Dancers RLR, LRL, RLR, Turn LRL), 16 cts.
3. Front Camel Walk, Face F, Out, Back, In, Turn Out (i.e. R-Dancers RLR, LRL, RLR, Turn LRL), 16 cts

Lead w/Outside Hip: Dancers on R side lead w/R hip, Dancers on L side lead w/L hip

4. Figure 8 circle back, 2X 4 cts. each, Travel Out, 8 cts.
   a.) Hip Circle, In-Front-Out-Back (i.e. R-Dancers RFLB), 4 cts.
   b.) Rib Circle, In-Front-In-Out-Back (i.e. R-Dancers RFLB), 4 cts.

Lead w/Inside Hip: Hip Dancers on R side lead w/L hip, Dancers on L side lead w/R hip

5. Figure 8 circle front, 2X 4 cts. each, Travel Out, 8 cts.
   a.) Hip Circle, Out-Front-In-Back (i.e. R-Dancers LFRB), 4 cts.
   b.) Rib Circle, Out-Front-In-Back (i.e. R-Dancers LFRB), 4 cts.

Lead w/Inside Foot: Dancers on R side lead w/L foot, Dancers on L side lead w/R foot

6. Snake Arms/Shoulder Rolls, w/Step-Together-Step, Travel S-S Inside to switch places, 8 cts.
7. Snake Arms/Shoulder Rolls, In place, Circle Out, then change weight, 8 cts.
8. Snake Arms w/Step-Together-Step, Travel S-S Inside to return to original side, 8 cts.
9. Snake Arms, In place, Circle Out, then change weight, 8 cts.

Lead w/Outside Foot: Dancers on R side lead w/R foot, Dancers on L side lead w/L foot

10. Front Camel Walk, Face F, In, Back, Out, Turn Out, **Untuck** the front veil flounce on Turn, 16 cts.
11. Front Camel Walk, Face F, Out, Back, In, w/veil in front; Turn Out, bring veil **long** edge overhead. 16 cts

Lead w/Outside Hip: Dancers on R side lead w/R hip, Dancers on L side lead w/L hip

12. Figure 8 circle back, w/veil long edge overhead, 2X 4 cts. each, Travel Out, 8 cts.
    a.) Hip Circle, In-Front-Out-Back, (i.e. R-Dancers LFRB), w/veil long edge overhead, 4 cts.
    b.) Rib Circle, In-Front-Out-Back, (i.e. R-Dancers LFRB), w/veil long edge overhead, 4 cts.

Lead w/Inside Hip: Hip Dancers on R side lead w/L hip, Dancers on L side lead w/R hip
    Figure 8 circle front, w/veil long edge overhead, 2X 4 cts. each, Travel Out, 8 cts.

    a.) Hip Circle, bring Out-Front-In-Back (i.e. R-Dancers RFLB), bring veil **short** edge overhead, 4 cts.
    b.) Rib Circle, Out-Front-In-Back (i.e. R-Dancers RFLB), bring veil short edge overhead, 4 cts.

Lead w/Inside Foot: Dancers on R side lead w/L foot, Dancers on L side lead w/R foot

13. Neck Slide w/Step-Together-Step, w/veil short edge overhead, Travel S-S Inside to switch places, 8 cts.

a.) Turn Out, **Untuck** the back veil flounce, bring veil in ***front***, In place, Circle Out, then change weight, 8 cts.

b.) Neck Slide w/Step-Together-Step, w/veil ***frame*** face, Travel S-S Inside to return to original side, 8 cts.

c.) Turn Out w/Veil in ***front***, In place, Circle Out, then put veil on R side for Matador, 8 cts.

Zig-Zag Floor Pattern: All Dancers lead w/R foot (Positions are RF RB LF LB):

1. Front Dancers do 3 Camels travel back w/Matador Arms; Back Dancers do 3 Camel travel front, RLR, LRL, RLR, Veil starts on R Arm, then Matador L, then Matador R arm, 12 cts.
2. Turn LRL, keep veil on R Arm, 4 cts.
3. Front Dancers do 3 Camels travel back w/Matador Arms; Back Dancers do 3 Camel travel front, RLR, LRL, RLR, Veil starts on R Arm, then Matador L, then Matador R arm, 12 cts.
4. Turn LRL, Switch veil to in back,.4 cts.

Lead w/Outside Foot: Dancers on R side lead w/R foot, Dancers on L side lead w/L foot, veil in ***back***

14. Camel Walk, F, In, Back, Out, Turn Out, (i.e. R-Dancers Flounce veil on RLR, Turn w/Veil Swirl RFLB, 16 cts.
15. Camel Walk, F, Out, Back, In, Turn Out, (i.e. R-Dancers Flounce veil on RLR, Turn w/Veil Swirl RFLB, 16 cts

Lead w/Outside Hip: Dancers on R side lead w/R hip, Dancers on L side lead w/L hip

16. Figure 8 circle back, w/veil in ***back***, 2X 4 cts. each, Travel Out, 8 cts.

a.) Hip Circle, In-Front-Out-Back, w/veil in back, (i.e. R-Dancers RFLB), 4 cts.

b.) Rib Circle, In-Front-In-Out-Back, w/veil in ***back***, (i.e. R-Dancers RFLB), 4 cts.

Lead w/Inside Hip: Hip Dancers on R side lead w/L hip, Dancers on L side lead w/R hip

17. Figure 8 circle front, w/veil in back, 2X 4 cts. each, Travel Out, 8 cts.

a.) Hip Circle, Out-Front-In-Back, w/veil in back, (i.e. R Dancers LFRB), 4 cts.

b.) Rib Circle, Out-Front-In-Back, w/veils in **back**, (i.e. R-Dancers LFRB), 4 cts.

Lead w/Inside Foot: Dancers on R side lead w/L foot, Dancers on L side lead w/R foot

18. Chasee Grapevine w/Veil Flounce, veil in **back** (i.e. R-Dancers LRL RLR LRL RLR, Veil RF LF RF LF), Travel S-S Inside to switch places, 8 cts.

a.) Veil Swirl Turn (i.e. R-Dancers LBRF), In place, Circle Out, then change weight, 8 cts.

19. Chasee Grapevine w/Veil Flounce, veil in **front** (i.e. R-Dancers RLR LRL RLR LRL, Veil LF RF LF RF), Travel S-S Inside return to original side, 8 cts.

b.) Veil Swirl Turn, (i.e. R-Dancers RBLF), In place, Circle Out, 8 cts.

20. End swirl w/Veil in **back**, do a few more turns Out, then do 2-3 **Airplane** Turns Out until music ends

21. **Pose** w/veil in back

DANCE NAZIRA *Meeny Yaba*, Finale

Dance was choreographed for group of 4 dancers, but a soloist can use the suggested steps and either dance in the audience or use floor patterns, such as squares or circles

Lead w/Inside Hip: Dancers on R side lead w/L hip, Dancers on L side lead w/R hip

1. Up & Down Hip Shimmy, In Place, Circle In, Arms D-U, U-D, (8 cts. w/o cymbals, 8 cts. w/ cymbals), 16 cts.

2. Ghawazee Floor Pattern, Twisting Hip Shimmy Arms Out 4 cts., Karshlimar Arms Up 4 cts., (16 cts. S-S, 16 cts. F/B, 16 cts. S-S, 16 cts. F/B), 64 cts.

3. Cross-Cross Arms Out 4 cts., Hip Drop-Drop Frame Hip 4 cts., Face Front, In, Back, Out, In Place, 32 cts.

4. Drum Solo # 1—Hip Vibration, In Place, Circle In, Arms D-U, U-D w/o cymbals, 16 cts.

5. V-Hip Thrusts, Travel In, w/**Inside Hip** to change sides, 16 cts.

Lead w/Outside Hip: Dancers on R side lead w/R hip, Dancers on L side lead w/L hip

1. Hip Thrust/Point Hand Out, face Aud., 2 cts, ½ Turn to F; Hip Thrust/Point Hand Out Back to Aud., 2 cts., use Outside Hip both times, 4 cts. Total
2. Twist Hip Shimmy Walk in ½ circle to face Aud. Use Outside Hip (same as 5a.), then change weight, 4 cts.
3. V-Hip Thrusts, Travel In, return to original side, 16 cts.

Lead w/Outside Hip: Dancers on R side lead w/R hip, Dancers on L side lead w/L hip

1. Hip Thrust/Point Hand Out, face Aud., 2 cts, ½ Turn to F; Hip Thrust/Point Hand Out Back to Aud., 2 cts., use Outside Hip both times, 4 cts. Total
2. Twist Hip Shimmy Walk in ½ circle to face Aud. Use Outside Hip (same as 5a.), 4 cts.
3. Drum Solo #2—Shoulder Shimmies, In Place, Circle In, Arms D-U, U-D w/o cymbals, 16 cts.
4. Ghawazee Floor Pattern, Twisting Hip Shimmy Arms Out 4 cts., Karshlimar Arms Up 4 cts., (16 cts. S-S, 16 cts. F/B, 16 cts. S-S, 16 cts. F/B), 64 cts.
5. Up & Down Hip Shimmy, In Place, Circle In, Arms D-U, U-D, 6 cts.
6. Turn, In Place Circle In, until drums stop

Performer Dance # 2

SAHARA CITY, Egyptian Cabaret Solo dance
Choreographed in 1992, music by *Belly Dance for Arabian Nights*

Veil Entrance

1. Enter from offstage w/veil in back, walk in circle;
2. Veil swirls, airplane turn, then get rid of veil;
3. Discard veil on back of stage, pose with back to aud., both arms down.

Sahara City
4/4 Section

1. a. Hip shimmy in place—8 cts., w/back to aud., arms down then come up
   b. Hip shimmy in place—8 cts., face aud., arms up then down

2. a. Walking Hip shimmy in circle to R—16 cts.
   b. Turn to R—16 cts.
   c. Walking Hip shimmy in circle to L—16 cts.
   d. Turn to L—16 cts.

3. a. Karshlimar step w/shimmy to L—16 cts., R foot leads
   b. Hip Thrusts—16 cts., face FLBR (RRLR, LLRL, RRLR, LLRL)
   c. Karshlimar step w/shimmy to R—16 cts., L foot leads
   d. Hip Thrusts—16 cts., face FRBL (LLRL, RRLR, LLRL, RRLR)

4. a. Tush Push to L—16 cts., (PSSS, PSSS, PSSS, PSSS)
   b. Point Step—3 times, face FBF)

5. a. Crossover Step-Hip Drop/Drop—16 cts. to R, in 1/2 circle to back
   b. 3/4 Shimmy Turn (end with back to aud.)

6. a. Backward Hip Thrusts—16 cts., 4 cts. each side (RLRL)
   b. R arm swoop, L arm swoop, both arms sweep (with back to aud.)

7. a. Basic Karshlimar—16 cts., face BRFL, R foot leads
   b. Turn—8 cts.

Beledi Section

1. a. L Hip Drops in circle—32 cts. (DDLDL DDLDL DDLDL DDLDL)

2. a. Basic Beledi to R—4 cts.
    b. Basic Beledi to L—4 cts.
    c. Turn-2-3 to R—4 cts.
    d. Turn-2-3 to L—4 cts.
    e. Basic Beledi to R—4 cts.
    f. Basic Beledi to L—4 cts.
    g. Turn-2-3 to R—4 cts.
    h. Turn-2-3 to L—4 cts.

3. a. Camel walk face F—4 cts., R foot leads
    b. Camel walk face R—4 cts., L foot leads
    c. Camel walk face B—4 cts., R foot leads
    d. Camel walk face L—4 cts., L foot leads

4. a. Hip Thrusts R—2 cts.
    b. Hip Thrusts L—2 cts.
    c. Turn 2-3/rib drop—3 cts.
       Bounce step in place, for music transition

5. a. Camel walk face F—4 cts., L foot leads
    b. Camel walk face L—4 cts., R foot leads
    c. Camel walk face B—4 cts., L foot leads
    d. Camel walk face R—4 cts., R foot leads

6. a. Hip Thrusts L—2 cts.
    b. Hip Thrusts R—2 cts.
    c. Turn 2-3/rib drop—3 cts.
       Bounce step in place, for music transition

7. a. Basic Beledi to R—4 cts.
    b. Basic Beledi to L—4 cts.
    c. Turn-2-3 to R—4 cts.
    d. Turn-2-3 to L—4 cts.
    e. Basic Beledi to R—4 cts.
    f. Basic Beledi to L—4 cts.
    g. Turn-2-3 to R—4 cts.
    h. Turn-2-3 to L—4 cts.

8. a. Camel walk face F—4 cts., R foot leads
    b. Camel walk face R—4 cts., L foot leads
    c. Camel walk face B—4 cts., R foot leads
    d. Camel walk face L—4 cts., L foot leads

9. a. Hip Thrusts R—2 cts.
    b. Hip Thrusts L—2 cts.
    c. Turn 2-3/rib drop—3 cts.
        Bounce step in place, for music transition

10. a. Camel walk face F—4 cts., L foot leads
    b. Camel walk face L—4 cts., R foot leads
    c. Camel walk face B—4 cts., L foot leads
    d. Camel walk face R—4 cts., R foot leads

11. a. Hip Thrusts L—2 cts.
    b. Hip Thrusts R—2 cts. c. Turn 2-3/rib drop—3 cts.
        Bounce step in place, for music transition

12. Hip Shimmy in big circle—16 cts.

Mamie Section

1. a. Hip Thrusts—2 cts. slow to L, face aud.
    b. Hip Thrusts—2 cts. slow to R, " "
    c. Hip Thrusts—2 cts. slow to L, " "
    d. Hip Thrusts—2 cts. slow to R, " "
    e. Turn—4 cts. f. Cissy—5 times (RL RLR)

2. a. Hip Thrusts—2 cts. slow to L, face R
    b. Hip Thrusts—2 cts. slow to R, " "
    c. Hip Thrusts—2 cts. slow to L, " "
    d. Hip Thrusts—2 cts. slow to R, " "
    e. Turn—4 cts. f. Cissy—5 times (RL RLR)

3. a. Hip Thrusts—2 cts. slow to L, face aud.
    b. Hip Thrusts—2 cts. slow to R, " "
    c. Hip Thrusts—2 cts. slow to L, " "
    d. Hip Thrusts—2 cts. slow to R, " "
    e. Turn—4 cts. f. Cissy—5 times (RL RLR)

4. a. Hip Thrusts—2 cts. slow to L, face L
    b. Hip Thrusts—2 cts. slow to R, " "
    c. Hip Thrusts—2 cts. slow to L, " "
    d. Hip Thrusts—2 cts. slow to R, " "
    e. Turn—4 cts. f. Cissy—5 times (RL RLR)

5. a. Zar head turns—16 cts. circle to L
    b. Head toss down, then up, sharply—1 beat

Performer Dance #3

BADIA, Egyptian Cabaret Style, 4-Part Dance
Choreographed in 2001, music by Raqia Hassan, *Dalaa el Helween*

I.) *INSTRUMENTAL*

1.) Intro/Entrance
- a. 8 counts Intro, hold offstage w/o zills (= slow 4 times)
- b. 24 counts Walking Hip Shimmy w/zills to enter stage, 4 foot leads (= slow 12 steps)
- c. 12 counts Step-Together-Step w/Hip Thrust travel R in ½ circle to Back (RLR, LRL, RLR)
  4 counts Turn to L (LRL)
- d. 12counts Step-Together-Step w/Hip Thrust travel L in ½ circle to Front (RLR, LRL, RLR)
  4 counts Turn to L (LRL)

2.) Accent : Walk backwards 2 cts, then forward 4 cts, R foot leads
- a. 6 counts + Accent 2 cts: Shoulder Shimmy, face aud.
- b. 4 counts + Accent 2 cts: R Hip Drop, face R.
- c. 4 counts + Accent 2 cts: Hip Thrust L, R, back to aud.
- a. 4 counts + Accent 2 cts: Shoulder Shimmy, face L

3.) Side to Side
- a. 4 counts Grapevine L, R, L, R, travel to L side w/L Hip Thrust (Drew Carey)
- b. 4 counts Turn to L, LRLR
- c. 4 counts Figure 8 on R side, Clockwise on R side (feet RLRL), w/R Arm out
- d. 4 counts Jameela L leg lift in front; both arms Sunset inside then out

II.) *VOCAL*

1.)

a.	12 counts	L Hip Thrust "V" travel to L (facing aud.)
	4 counts	Turn to L (end up facing R)
b.	12 counts	R Hip Thrust "V" travel to B (face R)
	4 counts	Turn to R (end up facing aud.)
c.	12 counts	R Hip Thrust "V" w/Shoulder Shimmy travel to R (face aud.)
	4 counts	Turn to R (end up facing R)

    d.   12 counts   L Hip Thrust "V" travel to F (facing R)

            4 counts   Turn to L (end up facing aud.)

2.) Accent: Walk backwards 2 cts, then forward 4 cts, R foot leads
- a. 6 counts + Accent 2 cts: Shoulder Shimmy, face aud.
- b. 4 counts + Accent 2 cts: R Hip Drop, face R.
- c. 4 counts + Accent 2 cts: Hip Thrust L, R, back to aud.
- d. 4 counts + Accent 2 cts: Shoulder Shimmy, face L

3.) Side to Side
- a. 4 counts Grapevine L, R, L, R, travel to L side w/L Hip Thrust
- b. 4 counts Turn to L, LRLR
- c. 4 counts Figure 8 on R side, Clockwise on R side (feet RLRL), w/R Arm out
- d. 4 counts Jameela L leg lift in front; both arms Sunset inside then out
- e. 4 counts L Hip Thrust on L side, w/L Arm Inside Sunrise
- f. 4 counts R Hip Thrust on L side, w/R Arm Inside Sunrise
- g. 6 counts Walk backwards 2 cts, then forward 4 cts, R foot leads
- h. 2 counts Turn to L
- i. 2 counts L Hip Drop-Lift

QASR AL SHOQ, Veil Dance
Choreographed in 2001, music by Mokhtar al Said, (Classic Egyptian Dance Music), *Raks Sharki*

A.) *Intro Section*
1.) Figure 8* w/both arms up (* Figure 8 is clock-wise on R, counter-clock on L)
Figure 8* w/hip thrusts, bring both arms down
2.) Snake Arms on R side (shoulder level)
Snake Arms on L side (shoulder level)
Snake Arms in circle to R
3.) Walk forward w/Hip Thrust R, L, R, L, R, L (bring both arms up), 6 cts.

B.) *Chorus #1*
1.) Camel Walk face FRBL (Lead foot RLRL), 16 cts.
2.) Snake Arms travel to R, 12 cts.
Turn to R, 4 cts.
3.) Camel Walk face FLBR (Lead foot LRLR), 16 cts.
4.) Snake Arms travel to L, 12 cts.
Turn to L, 4 cts.

C.) *Sub-Chorus*
1.) L Hip drop-drop (both arms inside Sunset on L side), 2 cts.
R Hip drop-drop (both arms inside Sunset on R side), 2 cts.
Rib cage drop-drop (both arms from up to down at face level), 2 cts.
L Hip Lift travel in circle to L (both arms Sunset inside then out), 8 cts.

2.) R Hip thrust-thrust w/Figure 8* (R arm only—Sunrise on R side), 2 cts.
L Hip thrust-thrust w/Figure 8* (L arm only—Sunrise on L side), 2 cts.
R Hip thrust-thrust w/Figure 8*(Both arms—Sunrise on R side), 2 cts.
R Hip Lift travel in circle to R (both arms Sunset inside then out), 8 cts.
R Hip thrust-thrust w/Figure 8* (R arm only—Sunrise on R side), 2 cts.
Figure 8 on L hip, R hip, 2 cts.

D.) *Chorus #2 w/Cape*
1.) Camel Walk face FLBR (Lead foot LRLR) while removing cape, 16 cts.
2.) Cape Flounces travel to L w/cape in front, 12 cts.
Cape Turn to L, 4 cts.
3.) Camel Walk face FRBL w/cape in back w/Flounces (Lead foot RLRL), 16 cts.
4.) Cape Flounces travel to R w/cape in front, 12 cts.
Cape Turn to R, 4 cts.

E.) ***Discard Cape***
1.) Travel to stage back area, 4 cts. (close cape until at back, then open and drop)
2.) Discard cape w/shoulder shimmy, 4 cts.

F.) ***Finale Section***
1.) Snake Arm pose on R (arms down to up)
2.) Snake Arm pose on L (arms down to up)
3.) Snake Arm pose in F (arms down then up to eye level w/Snake Arm frame face/eyes then back)
4.) Walk w/back to aud., 4 cts. (go towards R then face aud.)
5.) Walk forward while doing R Arm Outside Sunset from L-R; then L Arm Outside Sunset from R-L,
   Both Arms Inside Sunset; then pose w/Both Arms up (hold pose until Drum Solo w/weight on R foot).

DAHLENA Drum Solo

Choreographed in 2001, music by Trans Arabian Sound Band, *Moon Over Cairo Vol. II*

1.) a.) L Hip Hold-Drop-Lift-Drop, 4 cts.
   b.) R Hip Hold-Drop-Lift-Drop, 4 cts.
   c.) Shoulder Shimmy Thrust R-L, 2 cts.

2.) a.) Karshlimar w/Hip Shimmy, face F, R foot leads, 4 cts.
   b.) Karshlimar w/Hip Shimmy, face L, R foot leads, 4 cts
   c.) Karshlimar w/Hip Shimmy, face B, R foot leads, 4 cts
   d.) Karshlimar w/Hip Shimmy, face R, R foot leads, 4 cts
   e.) Karshlimar w/Hip Shimmy, face R, R foot leads, 4 cts
   f.) L foot cross over R foot and pivot ½ R turn until back to aud., bring both arms up, 2 cts.

3.) a.) L Hip Drop-Lift-Drop w/back to aud., Look over L shoulder, bring L arm down, 4 cts.\
   b.) R Hip Drop-Lift-Drop w/back to aud., Look over R shoulder, bring R arm down, 4 cts
   c.) Rib cage Lift-Drop w/back to aud., 2 cts.
   d.) Shoulder Shimmy turn ¼ to L until facing R, 4 cts.

4.) a.) Shoulder Shimmy walk backwards diagonal on L side w/L Arm out, R Arm up, L foot leads, 6 cts.
      Tush Push R foot step back then L foot, 2 cts.
   b.) Shoulder Shimmy walk backwards diagonal on R side w/R Arm out, L Arm up, R foot leads, 6 cts.
      Tush Push L foot step back then R foot, 2 cts.
   c.) Head Lift pose facing aud, 1 ct.

5.) a.) L Hip Lift-Drop Thrust travel to L, L Arm out, R Arm up (do wrist circle after 2 cts.), 4 x 4 cts = 16 cts
   b.) Figure 8* w/Hip Shimmy travel to R, w/Arm Figure 8 hip level, lead w/R hip, 4 x 4 cts = 16 cts
   c.) L Hip Up-up, Down-down, w/paddle hands, face aud., travel back, 4 x 4 cts = 16 cts.
   d.) Rib Slide R-L/Thrust F-B w/Shoulder Shimmy, face aud., travel forward, 4 x 4 cts. = 16 cts.
   e.) Grapevine w/Hip Shimmy travel to R, Lead w/L Hip Thrust, 4 x 4 cts. = 16 cts.

f.) Rib Undulation w/Rib Shimmy, face R, travel to back, 4 x 4 cts. = 16 cts. g) R Hip Thrust "V" travel to R w/back to aud., R Arm out, L Arm up, look over LR LR LR LR shoulder, 4 x 4 cts = 16

h.) Rib Undulation w/Rib Shimmy, face B, L, F, R, B, until back to aud., 5 x 4 cts. = 20 cts.

i.) L Hip Drop-Lift, w/back to Aud., 2 cts.

6.) a.) ¾ Hip Shimmy w/back to Aud., L hip leads, w/Arms Inside Sunset then Outside, 8 cts.

b.) Hip Thrust w/back to Aud. (L side 5 cts., R side 4 cts., L side 4 cts., R side 4 cts., L side 3 cts.)

Start w/Both arms Inside Sunset, then look over shoulder and Thrust same Arm during Accents on 3, 5, 7, 9, 11, 13, 15, 17, 19

7.) a.) Up & Down Hip Shimmy w/back to Aud., Arm Figure 8 & look over shoulder on L, R, L R sides 2x4=8 cts

b.) ½ pivot to L Face Aud., Up & Down Hip Shimmy., Arm Figure 8 & look on L, R, L R sides, 7 cts

8.) a.) Jump turn to L until back to aud., both arms down, 4 cts.; Jump bring arms up, head pose, 4 cts.

b.) Jump turn to L until facing aud., both arms down, 4 cts.; Jump bring arms up, head pose, 4 cts.

9.) a.) Ummy Ummy travel in circle to L, R Arm Up, L Arm Down, 8 cts.

b.) Choo Choo Shimmy travel in circle to L, Both Arms Inside Sunset, then Out, 8 cts.

c.) Ummy Ummy travel in circle to L, R Arm Up, L Arm Down, 8 cts.

d.) Choo Choo Shimmy travel in circle to L, Both Arms Inside Sunset, then Out, 10 cts.

10.) a.) Turn to L, 4 times

b.) Vibration pose face aud., bring both arms down to up on last count

ADY EHNA AHOO, Finale Dance
Choreographed in 2001, music by Raqia Hassan, *Dalaa el Helween*

A.) *Instrumental Section*
1.) L Hip Drop in place w/o zills, 6 times

2.) L Hip Thrust "V" travel to L, 12 cts.
Neck Slide in place LRL, 3 cts.

3.) R Hip Thrust "V" travel to R, 12 cts.
Neck Slide in place RLR, 3 cts.

4.) Camel Walk RLR face F, 3 cts.
Camel Walk LRL face R, 3 cts.
Camel Walk RLR face B, 3 cts.
   Step-Together-Step w/hip thrust LRL face B, 3 cts. (Both arms do clockwise circle from bottom L)
   Step-Together-Step w/hip thrust RLR face L, 3 cts. (Both arms cont. clockwise circle)
   Step-Together-Step w/hip thrust LRL face F, 3 cts. (Both arms finish 1 complete circle at bottom L)

5.) Drum Roll Hip Shimmy in place Arms start bottom Sunset inside; then Sunset down outside

6.) L Hip Thrust "V" travel in circle to L, 12 cts.
Shoulder Shimmy in place face aud., 3 cts.

7.) R Hip Thrust "V" travel in circle to R, 12 cts.
Shoulder Shimmy in place face aud., 3 cts.

8.) Camel Walk RLR face F, 3 cts.
Camel Walk LRL face R, 3 cts.
Camel Walk RLR face B, 3 cts.
   Step-Together-Step w/hip thrust LRL face B, 3 cts. (Both arms do clockwise circle from bottom L)
   Step-Together-Step w/hip thrust RLR face L, 3 cts. (Both arms cont. clockwise circle)
   Step-Together-Step w/hip thrust LRL face F, 3 cts. (Both arms finish 1 complete circle at bottom L)

B.) ***Vocal Section***

1.) Hip Thrust w/R leg extended R, L (look R, L) 2 cts
Cross R over L, Step to L side w/L, 2 cts.
Walk backwards RL, then forward RL w/Shoulder Shimmy, 4 cts.

2.) Hip Thrust w/L leg extended L, R (look L, R) 2 cts
Cross L over R, Step to R side w/R, 2 cts.
Walk backwards LR, then forward LR w/Shoulder Shimmy, 4 cts.

3.) Turn to L, 2 cts.
L Hip Drop, 2 cts.

FINGER CYMBALS (optional), Suggestions

A. **Badia**

1.) 1-1234, 1-1234, 1-1234, 1-2 x 3 sets. @ Entrance
1-1234, 1-1234, 1-1234, 1-1234, 1-1234, 1-1234, 1-1234, 1-2 x 2 sets @ Step-Together-Step

2.) 1-1234, 1-1234, 1-1234, 1-2-3 x 1 set. @ Accent
1-1234, 1-1234, 1-1234, 1-2
1-1234, 1-1234, 1-1234, 1-2
1-1234, 1-1234, 1-1234, 1-2 x 3 sets @ Accent

3.) 1-1234, 1-2 x 12 cts @ Side to Side
1-2-3 @ 4 cts. @ Side to Side

4.) 1-1234, 1-1234, 1-1234, 1-1234, 1-1234, 1-1234, 1-1234, 1-2 x 64 cts. @ Vocal

5.) 1-1234, 1-1234, 1-1234, 1-2-3 x 32 cts. @ Accent

6.) 1-1234, 1-2 x 12 cts @ Side to Side
1-2-3 @ 16 cts. @ Side to Side
1-2 @ L Hip Drop

B.) **Ady Ehna Ahoo**

1.) 1-1234, 1-1234, 1-1234, 1-1234, 1-1234, 1-1234, 1 x 2 times @ L Hip Thrusts

2.) 1-1234, 1-2, 1-2; 1-1234, 1-2, 1-2; 1-1234, 1-2, 1-2; 1 x 3 times @ Camel Walks

3.) 1-2 Double x 3 times @ Step-Together-Step
Hold cymbals during drum roll

4.) 1-1234, 1-1234, 1-1234, 1-1234, 1-1234, 1-1234, 1 x 2 times @ L Hip Thrusts

5.) 1-1234, 1-2, 1-2; 1-1234, 1-2, 1-2; 1-1234, 1-2, 1-2; 1 x 3 times @ Camel Walks

6.) 1-2 Double x 3 times @ Step-Together-Step

7.) 1-2 Double x 8 cts @ Vocal

1-2 Double x 8 cts @ Vocal

8. 1-2-3-4-5-6-7 x 1 time @ Turn/Hip Drop

Performer Dance #4

> **RAQSET EL FADAA**, Cabaret Veil Entrance, Drum Solo, Finale
> Choreographed in 1993, music by Omar Korshid,
> *Guitar El Chark/Rhythms of the Orient*

D.) *Entrance Dance*: *Guitar el Chark*
1.) Enter after 1st "weird" note;
2.) Walk to stage, up stairs on right side;
3.) Veil turn to R w/veil in back; then turn to L w/veil in front; then turn to R w/veil in back at hip level
4.) Discard veil towards back of stage on right side
5.) Pose for taxim that is next

E.) *Taxim/Drums/Stage Dance/Taxim*: *Raqset el Fadaa*
   Part 1—Taxim:
1.) Vibration pose w/arms down-look down, then bring arms up on inside of body (look up when finished); end with temple hand pose
2.) Vibration w/head roll, rib circle, then w/hip figure 8; while bringing hands down on inside
3.) Vibration w/hip figure 8, keep hands down
4.) Vibration w/rib circle
5.) Lunge to R (R arm out, palm up, come in, go down), w/vibration
6.) Lunge to L (L arm out, palm up, come in, go down), w/vibration
7.) Lunge to R (both arms out, palm up, come in, go down), w/vibration
8.) Lunge to F (both arms out, palm up, come in to eyes), w/vibration
9.) Vibration w/hip figure 8
10.) Vibration w/rib circle
11.) Vibration rib undulation facing R

   Part 2—Drum Solo: Use Finger Cymbals (1 2 3 4, 1-2-3-4-5-6); Hips/then Ribs
1.) Hips Up & Down shimmy—4 cts. w/o zills; Rib Shimmy—4 cts.; face R w/zills
   Hips Up & Down shimmy—4 cts.; Rib Shimmy—4 cts.; face F
   Hips Up & Down shimmy—4 cts.; Rib Shimmy—4 cts.; face L
   Hips Up & Down shimmy—4 cts.; Rib Shimmy—4 cts.; face B
2.) Tush Push w/back to Aud—4 cts; Rib Shimmy face aud—4 cts.
   Tush Push w/back to Aud—4 cts; Rib Shimmy face aud—4 cts.
   Tush Push travel to L—4 cts; Rib Shimmy face back—4 cts.
   Tush Push travel to L—4 cts; Rib Shimmy face back—4 cts.
3.) Hip Shimmy walk—4 cts.; Rib Shimmy—4 cts; in circle to R

Hip Shimmy walk—4 cts.; Rib Shimmy—4 cts; in circle to R
Hip Shimmy walk—4 cts.; Rib Shimmy—4 cts; in circle to R
Vibration pose facing aud—8 cts. (w/finger cymbal trill)

4.) R Hip Thrust to R—4 cts.; Turn to R w/Rib Shimmy—4 cts.
R Hip Thrust to R—4 cts.; Turn to R w/Rib Shimmy—4 cts.
R Hip Thrust to R—4 cts.; Turn to R w/Rib Shimmy—4 cts.

5.) R Hip Thrust to aud—4 cts.; Turn to aud w/Rib Shimmy—4 cts.
R Hip Thrust to L (back to aud)—4 cts.; Full Turn w/Rib Shimmy—4 cts.
R Hip Thrust to L (back to aud)—4 ct; ½ Turn to face aud w/Rib Shimmy-4 ct.

6.) Karshlimar w/hip shimmy RLRL to F—4 cts.; Rib Shimmy—4 cts.
Karshlimar w/hip shimmy RLRL to L—4 cts.; Rib Shimmy—4 cts.
Karshlimar w/hip shimmy RLRL to B—4 cts.; Rib Shimmy—4 cts.
Karshlimar w/hip shimmy RLRL to R—4 cts.; Rib Shimmy—4 cts.

7.) Cha Cha step RL RLR to L—4 cts.; Rib Shimmy—4 cts.
Cha Cha step LR LRL to R—4 cts.; Rib Shimmy—4 cts.
Cha Cha step RL RLR to L—4 cts.; Rib Shimmy—4 cts.
Cha Cha step LR LRL to R—4 cts.; Rib Shimmy—4 cts.

8.) Hip Thrust in place RLR—4 cts.; Rib Shimmy—4 cts.
Hip Thrust w/leg extension RLR—4 cts.; Rib Shimmy—4 cts
Hip Thrust w/leg extension LRL—4 cts.; Rib Shimmy—4 cts

9.) Cher Jumps to R—2 times; Rib Shimmy w/camel arch back—4 cts.
Cher Jumps to L—2 times; Rib Shimmy w/camel arch back—4 cts.

10.) Pelvic Ummy (on toes, in place) face L—4 cts.; Rib circle face L—4 cts.
Pelvic Ummy (on toes, in place) face back to aud—4 cts.; Rib circle face aud—4 cts.
Pelvic Ummy (on toes, in place) face R—4 cts.; Rib circle face R—4 cts.

11.) Body Snake w/Vibration facing R (from bottom to top) w/zill trills
Maya—Pelvic Roll—Rib Roll—Head up—Hands to Sky—16 cts. ?

12.) Rib Drop face RR—step back—2 cts.
Rib Drop face LL—step back—2 cts.
Rib Drop face RR—step back—2 cts.
Rib Drop face LL—step back—2 cts.

13.) Turn to R—8 counts

Part 3—4/4 Stage Dance:

1.) Hip Thrust to R—4 times, (RRRR, LLLL, RRRR, LLLL), travel diagonally from back of stage to front of stage—16 cts.

2.) 3/4 Hip Twist—8 times (RLR, LRL, RLR, LRL, RLR, LRL, RLR LRL)—16 cts.

3.) L Arm Lunge to L in place—4 cts.

4.) Turn to L—4 cts.

5.) Hip Thrust to L—4 times, (RRRR, LLLL, RRRR, LLLL), travel diagonally from back of stage to front of stage—16 cts.

6.) 3/4 Hip Twist—8 times (LRL RLR, LRL, RLR, LRL, RLR, LRL, RLR)—16 cts.

7.) R Arm Lunge to R in place—4 cts.

8.) Turn to R—4 cts.

1.) Hip Thrust w/back to aud—4 times, (RRRR, LLLL, RRRR, LLLL), travel diagonally from back of stage to front of stage—16 cts.

2.) 3/4 Hip Twist—8 times (RLR, LRL, RLR, LRL, RLR, LRL, RLR)—16 cts.

3.) R Arm Lunge to R—4 cts.; then L Arm Lunge to L—4 cts.

4.) Turn to R—4 cts.

Part 4—*Taxim*:

1.) Start out facing R—hip circle, camel, backbend & snake arms; then snake arms to face L

2.) On L side do floor descent w/snake arms, standing snake arms & backbend pose

3.) Can do snake arms to face aud., or end w/backbend pose facing L

4.) Fix hair during long pause before drum solo

DRUM SOLO
Music by Samy Faraq, *Arabian Melodies*

F.) *Drum Solo*: Arabian Melodies

1.) Rib drops on L side-2 cts.
" " " R "-2 cts.
Hip drops on L side-2 cts.
" " " R"—2 cts.

2.) Walking hip shimmy-8 cts. (1/2 circle from face aud. to back to aud.)
Jump-1 ct./Hip shimmy in place-7 cts. (w/arms down then up)
Jump-1 ct to face aud./Hip shimmy in place-7 cts. (facing aud., w/ arms down then up)

3.) R foot step F, B, F, Turn-4 cts., (travelling to R side)
L foot step F, B, F, Turn-4 cts., (travelling to L side)

4.) Rib slide L, R, Rib thrust F, B-4 cts/Rib circle-2 cts./Hip ummy ummy-4 cts. (fast) (in place)
Rib slide L, R, Rib thrust F, B/Rib shimmy-5 cts. (fast) (in place)

5.) L Hip thrust-2 cts./Turn-2 cts. (to L side), 4 times-16 cts.

6.) Turn w/hip shimmy-10 cts. to R

7.) Hip circle w/vibration-?? cts.

8.) Rib drop in place-1 ct.

NADO, Finale Dance
Music by Music Arabian (Voice of Lebanon label, has Nagwa Fouad on cover), *Belly Dance Vol. 2*

G.) *Finale*: Nado
   * Drum Roll: Vibration pose in place w/finger cymbals

1.) Walk 24 cts. in square (4 cts. to R, 4 cts. to aud., 8 cts. to L, 4 cts. back, then 4 cts. to center back stage)

2.) Turn to R—20 cts.

3.) Zar turn to L—16 cts.

4.) R hip thrust w/leg extend—4 cts; L hip thrust w/leg extend—4 cts.; Rib drop-lift/drop drop face R—4 cts; Rib drop-lift/drop drop face L—4 cts

5.) Crossover step w/Hip Drop to R,—12 cts. (RLdrop/drop, LRdrop/drop, RLdrop/drop); Turn to L—4 cts.
    Push step back—12 cts. (RLR, LRL, RLR); Turn to R—4 cts.

6.) Crossover step w/Hip Drop to L,—12 cts. (RLdrop/drop, LRdrop/drop, RLdrop/drop); Turn to L—4 cts.
    Push step back—12 cts. (RLR, LRL, RLR); Turn to R—4 cts.

7.) Walk to R—4 cts.; Zar head turn—4 cts
    Walk to L—4 cts.; Zar head turn—4 cts

8.) Crossover step w/Hip Drop to R,—12 cts. (RLdrop/drop, LRdrop/drop, RLdrop/drop); Turn to L—4 cts.
    Push step back—12 cts. (RLR, LRL, RLR); Turn to R—4 cts.

9.) Crossover step w/Hip Drop to L,—12 cts. (RLdrop/drop, LRdrop/drop, RLdrop/drop); Turn to L—4 cts.
    Push step back—12 cts. (RLR, LRL, RLR); Turn to R—4 cts.

10.) 3/4 Hip Shimmy in place w/arm circle—8 cts.

11.) Fast Walk in Circle to R—16 cts.; Turn—6 cts.
    Fast Walk in Circle to L—16 cts.; Turn—6 cts. (w/zar optional); Pose!

Performer Dance #5

Rugisnee, Cape Entrance, Stage Dance, Drum Solo Finale
Choreographed in 1992, music by Raja Zahr, *Raja's Dancer's Paradise &*
Disco Balady

ENTRANCE DANCE TO RUGISNEE:
1. Intro—8 cts., hold offstage
2. Walk onto stage with veil draped in front & behind body, 4 sets—8 cts. each (music is same as #1)
3. Turn to R—8 cts., w/veil in back
   Airplane to R—8 cts., "
   Turn to R—8 cts.,　　　 "
   Airplane to R—8 cts., "
4. Open/Close Veil w/back to Aud.—4 cts. forward, 4 cts. back*
   Open/Close Veil on Left side—4 cts. forward, 4 cts. back*
   Open/Close Veil Facing Aud.—4 cts. forward, 4 cts. back*
   Open/Close Veil on Right side—4 cts. forward, 4 cts. back*
   *w/Basic Walk, either RLR-hold or LRL-hold
5. Open/Close Veil shoulder level facing Aud—8 cts, w/Hip Shimmy in place
   Open/Close Veil above head facing Aud.—8 cts., w/Hip Shimmy in place
6. Discard Veil (behind you)—4 cts. (end with both arms up)

7. **1st Set of Voices**:
a. Maya (bring both arms down)—4 cts.,
b. Hand shakes to R—4 cts.; keep hands hip level, travel forward
c. Maya (bring both arms up)—4 cts.,
d. L Arm w/Lunge on L—4 cts.; keep hands hip level, travel forward
e. Maya (bring both arms down)—4 cts.,
f. Hand shakes to R—4 cts.; keep hands hip level, travel forward
g. Maya (bring both arms up)—4 cts.,

8. Up & Down Hip Shimmy in place (bring both arms down)—3 cts; fast body wave bring both arms up—1 ct.

9. a. Turn to R (arms up/down/up)—4 cts.
   b. Turn to L (arms up/down/up)—4 cts.
   c. Hip Thrust to R (bring both arms down)—4 cts.
   d. Hip Thrust to R w/back to aud. (bring both arms up)—4 cts.

10. a. Karshlimar w/Hip Shimmy face aud. (arms forward then up to face)—4 cts.,
    b. Karshlimar w/Hip Shimmy back to aud. (arms up)—4 cts.

11. a. Hip thrust w/back to aud (arms diagonal up 4 times)—4 cts., use Soheir Zaki Hips with 3/4 shimmy
    b. Hip thrust w/back to aud (arms diagonal down 4 times)—4 cts., use Soheir Zaki Hips with 3/4 shimmy
    c. Same hip movement travel to R—4 cts. (hand accent at end)
    d. Same hip movement travel to L—4 cts. (hand accent at end)

12. a. Rib Circle/Hip Ummy/Rib Circle/Body Wave up—4 cts. slow
    b. Maya/Maya/Pelvic Circle up—4 cts. fast
    c. 3/4 Hip shimmy travel until back to aud.—8 cts.

13. a. Double hip thrusts w/Back to aud, 4 sets—2 cts.; R arm out/down, L arm out/down, R arm sweep out/up, L arm sweep out/up (Hips-RR LL RR LL)
    b. Double hip thrusts Face R, 4 sets—2 cts.; Both arms trace body from up to down (Hips-RR LL RR LL)
    c. Double hip thrusts Face aud, 4 sets—2 cts.; R arm out/down, L arm out/down, R arm sweep out/up, L arm sweep out/up (Hips-RR LL RR LL)
    d. Double hip thrusts Face L, 4 sets—2 cts.; Both arms trace body from up to down (Hips-RR LL RR LL)
    e. Figure 8 w/up & down hip shimmy facing aud.—8 cts.

14. **Voices Say**: *"Make Me Dance Slowly, little by little"*
    a. Rib Shimmy w/arms close/open to R side, travel forward
    b. Rib Shimmy w/arms close/open to L side, travel forward
    c. Rib Shimmy w/arms close/open to R side, travel forward
    d. Rib Shimmy w/arms close/open to L side, travel forward
    e. Rib Shimmy w/lunge to R in place
    f. Rib Shimmy w/lunge to L in place
    g. Rib Shimmy w/lunge up in place
    h. Rib Shimmy w/lunge down (touch floor)

15. a. Turn to R—4 cts.
    b. Zar head turn to L—16 cts.
    c. Karshlimar face aud.—4 cts. (arms sweep up)
    d. Karshlimar back to aud.—4 cts. (arms trace body down)
    e. Karshlimar face aud.—4 cts. (arms sweep up)

f. Hip Thrust to R face aud.—4 cts (bring arms down)

g. Hip Thrust to R back to aud—4 cts (bring arms up)

16. a. Shoulder Shimmy Lunge forward face R—2 cts.

b. Shoulder Shimmy Lunge forward face F—2 cts.

c. Shoulder Shimmy Lunge forward face L—2 cts.

d. Shoulder Shimmy Lunge forward face B—2 cts.

e. Shoulder Shimmy walk in circle w/R hand points—2 cts.

f. Shoulder Shimmy walk in circle w/R hand points—2 cts.

g. Shoulder Shimmy walk in circle w/R hand points—2 cts.

h. Shoulder Shimmy walk in circle w/R hand points—2 cts.

i. Shoulder Shimmy walk in circle w/R hand points—2 cts.

j. Turn to L—4 times (2 cts. each)

k. Head Roll—2 cts.

YANI Drum Solo
Choreographed in 1995, music by Raja Zahr, *Disco Balady*

SECTION W/O ZILLS:

1.) Rib Lift/Hip Down Section

   a.) Rib Lift drop, face diagonal R, 2 cts.

   b.) Rib Lift drop, face diagonal L, 2 cts.

   c.) L Hip Down up down, face diagonal L, 3 cts. (5 ct. hold)

   d.) R Hip Down up down, face diagonal R, 3 cts. (5 ct. hold) e.) L Hip Down up down, face aud. w/both arms up, 3 cts. (5 ct. hold)

2.) Hip Drop Front side back side Section

   a.) L Hip Drop FSBSFS, face F, 8 cts. (then head lift)

   b.) L Hip Drop FSBSFS, face R diagonal, 8 cts.

   c.) L Hip Drop FSBSFS, face B, both hands down, 8 cts.

   d.) R Hip Drop FSBSFS, face B, both hands down, 8 cts.

3.) Back to Audience (hands start down)/Transition Section

   a.) 3/4 Hip Shimmy in place w/back to aud. hand D U, 4 cts.

   b.) 3/4 Hip Shimmy in place w/back to aud. hand U D, 4 cts.

   c.) 1/2 Turn to R, fast, then walk to Aud., 8 cts.
     (Bring R hand up on 5th ct., then L hand)

4.) Hip Down/Turn Section

   a.) Reda Hip Down, travel to R, (Palms up, down, up, down), 8 cts.
     (hip down goes front, back, front, back slowly)

b.) 3/4 Shimmy to R in Circle, 3 cts., Arms inside Sunset, (change weight on 4)

c.) Reda Hip Down, travel to L, (Palms up, down, up, down), 8 cts. (hip down goes front, back, front, back slowly)

d.) 3/4 Shimmy to L in Circle, 3 cts., Arms inside Sunset, (change weight on 4)

e.) 3/4 Shimmy Walk to Back, Arms from Up to Down, 4 cts.

f.) 3/4 Shimmy Walk to Back (w/back to aud), Arms from Down to Up, 4 cts.

g.) Hip Thrusts in place RLRL (w/back to aud.) & Wrist Slides RLRL, 4 cts.

5.) Backward L Floor Pattern (start at Center Stage Back)

a.) Hold 2, then Rib Undulate w/Shoulder Shimmy, travel to L (face R), 6 cts.

b.) Shoulder Shimmy turn in place to R, 1/2 times, 8 cts.

c.) Rib Undulate w/Shoulder Shimmy, travel to R (face L), 8 cts.

d.) Shoulder shimmy with Rib Slide R L/Lift drop; Rib Slide R L/ Lift drop travel forward, 8 cts. (hands hip level)

6.) Shoulder Shimmy/Kick & Jump/Hip Thrust Section

a.) Shoulder Shimmy/Kick on diagonal R, both arms out, 4 cts.

b.) Shoulder Shimmy/Kick on diagonal L, both arms out, 4 cts.

c.) Shoulder Shimmy/Kick on diagonal R, bring R hand to face, 4 cts.

d.) Shoulder Shimmy/Kick on diagonal L, bring both hand up, 4 cts.

7.) Hip Thrust "W" FSBS Section

a.) Hip Thrust "W" face F, 4 cts.

b.) Hip Thrust "W" face R, 4 cts.

c.) Hip Thrust "W" face B, 4 cts.

d.) Hip Thrust "W" face L, 4 cts.

d.) Hip Thrust "W" face F, 4 cts.

8.) Jump/Hip Thrust Traveling Forward Section

a.) Jump/R Hip Thrust on R, extend R arm, 4 cts.

b.) Jump/R Hip Thrust on L, extend L arm, 4 cts.

c.) Jump/R Hip Thrust on R, extend both arms, 4 cts.

9.) Shimmy/Tush Push/Snap Section

a.) Shimmy Walk to Center stage back w/back to aud., 4 cts.

b.) L Hip Thrust Walk travel to L w/back to aud 4 times, 16 cts. (look behind L shoulder, every 4 cts.)

c.) Tush Push w/shimmy in complete Circle to R, 8 cts.
d.) Look behind L shoulder, do shoulder snap F/B, 2 cts.
e.) Look behind R shoulder, do shoulder snap F/B, 2 cts.

10.) Run/Drop/Shimmy Section
a.) Bounce walk/Run to Center Stage back, 4 cts.
b.) Rib drop facing L 4 times, 4 cts.
c.) Bounce walk/Run to Center Stage front, 4 cts.
d.) Rib drop facing R 4 times, 4 cts.

11.) Clap/Shoulder Shimmy Section
a.) Clap, then shoulder shimmy on L side, arms open on L, 4 cts.
b.) Clap, then shoulder shimmy on R side, arms open on R, 4 cts.
c.) Shoulder shimmy in vertical 1/2 circle under from L R, 4 cts.
d.) Shoulder shimmy in vertical 1/2 circle under from R L, 4 cts.

12.) Rib Undulate Sections
a.) Walk back (or vibrate in place?), facing aud., 4 cts.
b.) Rib Undulate on R side, bring L hand down, 4 cts.
c.) Rib Undulate on L side, bring R hand down, 4 cts.
d.) Rib Undulate facing aud., bring both hand down, 4 cts.

13.) Section I Finale
a.) Walk forward, arms inside Sunset, 4 cts.
b.) 3/4 Hip Shimmy, turn in circle to R, 8 cts.
c.) R Hip Drop in Circle to R, 12 cts.

SECTION WITH ZILLS: **Optional**

14.) a.) Turn to L w/Zar head, slow, 8 cts.
b.) Hold, bring both arms up, 2 cts. (hold cymbals 2 cts.)

15.) a.) Cher Jump/bounce face L (bring arms U D), 4 cts.
b.) Cher Jump/bounce face R (bring arms U D), 4 cts.
c.) Cher Jump/bounce face Front (bring arms U D), 4 cts.

16.) a.) Hold face aud., 4 cts.
b.) Ummy ummy face F/jump turn face B, 4 cts.
c.) Ummy ummy face B/jump turn face F, 4 cts.
d.) Ummy ummy face F, 4 cts.

17.) a.) 3/4 Shimmy Travel in Circle from R to L, 20 cts.
    b.) Ummy ummy in place face aud., 4 cts.

18.) a.) Walk back, 3 cts.
    b.) R Arm extend to R, 2 cts.
    c.) Walk back, 4 cts.
    d.) L Arm extend to L, 2 cts.
    e.) Rib drop pose on R, 2 cts.
    f.) Rib drop pose on L, 2 cts.
    g.) Pelvic Tuck pose on R, 1 ct.
    h.) Pelvic Turk pose on L, 1 ct.

19.) a.) Rib Drop Pose face R w/level change up/down/up/down, 11 cts.
    b.) Turn to L, back to aud., 1 ct.

20.) a.) Hip Shimmy in place RLRL, bring both arms from U D, back to aud., 4 cts.
    b.) R Hip Extend to R, on L side, back to aud, 4 cts.
    c.) R Hip Extend to R, on R side, face aud, 4 cts.
    d.) R Hip Extend to R, on L side, back to aud, 4 cts.
    e.) R Hip Extend to R, forward, face aud, 4 cts.
    f.) R Hip Extend to R, back, back to aud, 4 cts.
    g.) R Hip Extend to R, forward, face aud, 4 cts.

21.) a.) Walk back, back to aud, 4 cts.
    b.) Walk forward, face aud., 4 cts.
    c.) Walk in small circle from L to R, 8 cts.

22.) a.) Turn to L in Circle, do zar turn after 8, 8 cts.
    b.) Turn to L in Circle, do zar turn after 4, 4 cts.
    c.) Turn to L in Circle, do zar turn after 4, 4 cts.

23.) a.) Turn to L in Circle, 12 cts.
    b.) turn to L in Circle w/zar head, 12 cts.

24.) a.) Vibration in place b.) Collapse/up, 1 ct.

PERFORMER DANCE EXAMINATION & CHECKLIST

Student Name: _____

Instructor Name: _____

Exam Date: _____

1. Name five (5) different Belly Dance styles:

    a. _____

    b. _____

    c. _____

    d. _____

    e. _____

2. What is Choreography? _____

    What is Free Style? _____

3. Name five rhythm accompaniments, identify which 2 are "natural":

    a. _____

    b. _____

    c. _____

    d. _____

    e. _____

4. Name 5 of your favorite Belly Dance DVDs or Videos, some you already own or search the internet for this answer:

    a. _____

    b. _____

    c. _____

    d. _____

    e. _____

5. Name three nationally known Middle Eastern musicians who have recorded albums or tapes, include the name of their album or tape for extra credit:

    a. _____

    b. _____

    c. _____

6. Name five "specialty dances" that involve the use of "Props":

    a. _____

    b. _____

    c. _____

d. _____

e. _____

7. Balance techniques (name 5 places a cane or sword can be balanced on:

a. _____

b. _____

c. _____

d. _____

e. _____

8. What can cane dancing consist of:

a. _____

b. _____

c. _____

9. A "Cabaret Dance" can consist of six different parts, name and describe them:

a. _____

b. _____

c. _____

d. _____

e. _____

f. _____

10. Give a finger cymbal pattern that can be used with the following rhythms:

a. 44 _____

b. 9/8 _____

c. beledi _____

Dance Performance Checklist, the student must perform the following dances before completing all levels:

Performer Level

1. Dance Ramza/Selma/Nazira, cabaret entrance, veil & finale
2. Sahara City, veil or cape entrance w/finger cymbals
3. Badia, Egyptian Cabaret
4. Faqset el Fadaa, Veil, stage dance, finale
5. Rugisnee, cape dance, Yani drum solo
6. Assignment: Choreograph a 5-Part Dance Routine that is 8-10 Minutes Long

CHOREOGRAPHY, FREE STYLE & STYLE

CHOREOGRAPHY: is the art of creating and arranging dances-basically. When done well, the result will be a seemingly effortless, inspiring performance combining good use of space, skill, positioning, and uniformity of movement.

To choreograph or not to choreograph will be determined by:

- Type of dance,
- Style of dancer(s),
- Skill of dancer(s),
- Performance setting, etc.

1. TYPE OF DANCE:
   Choreography works best for some types of dance such as ballet, tap, jazz, Egyptian Oriental, etc., but might not be a necessity for others such as break dance, disco dance, and some forms of middle eastern dance.

2. STYLE OF DANCER(S):
   The individual styles of the dancer(s) can determine whether or not to choreograph also. Like so many other dance forms, middle eastern dance offers various styles to choose from: Turkish, Egyptian Pharonic, Greek, etc., with individual decisions being made about whether choreography is appropriate for that particular style.

3. SKILL OF DANCER(S):
   A lot of "beginning" performers like the "security" of knowing where each step falls in relationship to the music, but on the other hand—a well-seasoned veteran performer might enjoy the challenge of performing "free style" with a live band.

4. PERFORMANCE SETTING:
   Where will you perform this routine: a theatre stage indoors, an outdoor festival, a child's birthday party, a home party, an office celebration, etc.?

Is it easier or more difficult to choreograph a routine for yourself or someone else? (If it's yourself—you know your own style, skills and limitations very well; but if it's for someone else—you'll need to consider their dance skills, personality, and "body types.")

WHERE TO BEGIN:

1. Observe other dancers-via TV, videos, live shows, etc.
   - Watch floor patterns, movements and how it relates to music
   - Start a "Video Library" of your favorite dance productions
   - Check out books/videos from library on dance/choreography

2. Select your music:
   - What is the mood/look/style you want to create/project?
   - Which songs excite you, move you to dance

3. Consider costuming for your choreographed piece:
4. Consider performance setting
5. Consider who will perform it-you, a troupe, students, etc.
6. Know your music:
   - Listen to it over and over again
   - Note the tempo or rhythm changes
   - What mood does it invoke?
   - How does the music rise and fall?

7. Write down a basic "beat" structure for drums or melody section for slow music
   - Count per count, beat per beat, measure per measure, when using drum rhythms
   - For a taxim, you can note when the nai begins, whether it is a long or short note, does the music have vocals, is the music structured or more free style?

8. Which steps fit the music:
   - Fast or slow steps
   - Large or small steps
   - Travelling or stationary steps
   - High or lowered steps

9. What floor patterns look best with steps and music:
   - *Circles, squares, diagonal lines, triangles, lines, etc.

10. Combine costuming, setting, performers, music, beats, steps and floor patterns into the final product: THE CHOREOGRAPHED DANCE.

Beginners may wish to start with a short routine (1-3 min.); Intermediate or Advanced students might choreograph a 3-5 min. dance for a seminar show; Advanced students and Performers might choreograph a 5-7 min. dance for a BellyGram; and Performers might sketch out or choreograph a longer 10-15 or 20 min. dance for a Restaurant, Nightclub or Show.

FREE STYLE

A discussion of Choreography would not be complete without mentioning its opposite: "Free Style."

Free Style (or "Winging It") involves performing steps and/or finger cymbals, veils, etc. to a known rhythm or song without the benefit of knowing what steps or combinations to do beforehand.

Free Style can be both challenging to the performer and exciting to the audience. (Can you tell when a dancer is performing a choreographed routine—or when they're performing "free style"?) Free Style also involves preparation beforehand—you must know basic rhythms, steps, and finger cymbal patterns—it doesn't give you an excuse to do "anything" onstage, you'll still need to think about what to do with your veil, whether or not you'll do sword dancing, floor work or taxim, etc.

Try doing a one-minute dance "Free Style", then choreograph steps to it—which method do you prefer?

CHOREOGRAPHY VS. FREE STYLE

- Choreography involves careful, well-thought out "preparations" for a particular dance movement, routine, or performance.
- Free Style involves preparation of a different nature—knowing what you're going to do onstage without exact details regarding steps.

DANCE ESSENTIALS

Dance ability (the ability to execute steps, move to various rhythms, use various props, play finger cymbals or other accompaniments, etc.) is an absolute necessity in order for one to become a professional dance performer!

But, to top that off, one needs "icing on the cake" or other DANCE ESSENTIALS! Proper costuming that fits the dance, having your dance tell a story, making sure you're CD or cassette is recorded perfectly, Stage Make-up, Stage Hair, Showmanship, Professionalism and good Business sense should be considered along the way to becoming a professional dance performer!

STYLE

1. What is "Style"? A definition could be an individualized "way" or method of expressing something, whether it's dancing, singing, acting, designing clothes or costumes, etc.
2. What comes to mind when you think about style? Usually, I think of individuality—wouldn't it be boring if all dancers did the same routine with the same costume, same music, same expressions, etc. every time you saw a Belly Dancer? Yes, it would be very boring indeed. The same thing applies to singers, actors, and fashions.

INDIVIDUALITY IS THE KEY TO STYLE that adds "spice" to self-expression.

3. What are ways to obtain an individual "style"? There are many ways-for example watching other dancers—and asking yourself what you like and dislike about their dance performance; listening to any and every kind of Belly Dance song you can get your hands on; attending dance seminars to get new and FRESH ideas in choreography, steps, costuming, etc. and MOST IMPORTANT OF ALL: cutting the "apron strings" from your teacher's style—this takes TIME and a lot of COURAGE, but it's something that you have to do if you want to become "YOUR OWN" performer.

Be an individual—BE YOURSELF—the greatest secret to being a great dancer is doing something that no other dancer can do: DANCE LIKE YOU!!!

Of course however, you should be aware that the word "style" has a dual meaning: one referring to individuality—the other referring to a "set" way of expressing oneself in Belly Dance. Dancers are often typecast as having a certain(s) "style" or "method" of performing: which can fit into some main categories:

1. Cabaret
2. Ethnic/Folkloric
3. Specialty

Some dancers also combine these three elements, i.e. Ethno-Cabaret, or a Specialty dance performed in either cabaret or ethnic costuming, etc.

"Style" sub-categories are more specialized: denoting a specific country, area, "type of costume/music/step", or "term", for example:

1. Greek style
2. Turkish style
3. Arabic style
4. Persian style
5. Lebanese style
6. North African style
7. Armenian style
8. Egyptian style
9. Oriental style
10. Moroccan style and the list goes on and on and on.

Other terms come to mind when considering and describing a particular dance style—for example: flirty, shy, bold, dramatic, etc. (Some of these terms can be "cross-referenced" with "Dance Mood".) Which one(s) can you project?

Although "generic" dance styles are available to choose from—these title have nothing to do with your individualized/personalized "Dance Style". What is your "Dance Style"? Can you perform one or several? Be aware of the various styles.

YOUR CHOREOGRAPHED DANCE ROUTINE
What kind of dance would you like to create?

If you have been watching belly dances available on YouTube, MySpace the internet or through videos, you have noticed various different dance styles.

You may view one dance that is cabaret style, with a flashy skirt, bra & belt using finger cymbals (zills); or you might notice a "goth" style dance that uses heavy rhythms performed in dance pants. Or perhaps you viewed a traditional cane dance routine performed in a Beledi dress. You may have also seen dances performed in person, perhaps at a Greek restaurant that included a Karshlimar with skirt flounces or at a RenFair with troupes dancing with swords, baskets, tambourines, etc.

What about dance rhythms? You can also do some research on the internet by viewing the CD or album song info. Many of the belly dance music CDs will actually tell you the name of the song, i.e. *Raks Leyla* and mention that it has Beledi and Chiftitelli rhythms in the song.

What are some favorite dance steps that you would like to include, such as hip circle, walking hip shimmy, shoulder shimmy, arm circles, etc. Is the tempo slow, fast or medium? Will you include a veil or finger cymbals in your dance?

How do you plan to use the dance floor? If you picked Hip circle, will you perform that in place or use traveling hip circles? If you choose to use a shoulder shimmy, is it in place or travelling? If you plan to travel with a step, will you dance from left to right, front to' back, in a circle, square or zig zag pattern?

Once you have idea and a song picked out, next you want to listen to the song over and over again to notice the rhythm patterns, music changes, tempo, etc.

In Belly Dance, you have the freedom to choose whatever dance style you like and the freedom to choose the dance song and rhythm that speaks to you.

Your choreographed routine can contain the following elements that could be used in a Cabaret Dance suitable for a restaurant show:

1. Entrance dance
2. Veil dance
3. Specialty, stage dance or visit audience
4. Floor dance and/or taxim
5. Drum solo
6. Finale

Note that you are not limited to using a "cabaret" style dance; you can create a folkloric dance instead and include the elements of Cane Dance, Sword, Tambourine, etc.

You must use different rhythms for the different parts of the routine—for example, don't use chiftitelli for every section.

Length: Can be anywhere from 8 to 10 minutes—the choice is up to you and contain at least 3 or 5 different sections

Costume: Must reflect the style of your dance and match the music.

Notes: Must be provided for your routine (typed or neatly handwritten).

Thoughts on creating a "personalized" dance routine —write down your favorites:

Style:	Moods:
Costume(s):	Dancers:
Colors:	Routines:
Rhythms:	Props:
Music:	Other Thoughts:
Songs:	

Here are some questions to consider for your choreography:

Name of Dance: _____

Name of Song(s): _____

Artist/CD/LP: _____

Style of Dance _____

Dance Length/Total Sections: _____

Use Finger Cymbals, Veil, Cape or other Props? _____

Section 1 (Entrance): _____

Rhythm(s): _____

Use Finger Cymbals?: _____

Steps to include: _____

Section 2 (Veil/Slow): _____

Rhythm(s): _____

Use Veil/Cape?: _____

Steps to include: _____

Section 3 (Medium): _____

Rhythm(s): _____

Use Finger Cymbals?: _____

Steps to include: _____

Section 4 (Taxim/Floor Work): _____

Rhythm(s): _____

Use Finger Cymbals?: _____

Steps to include: _____

Section 5 (Drum Solo): _____

Rhythm(s): _____

Use Finger Cymbals?: _____

Steps to include: _____

_____

Section 6 (Finale): _____

Rhythm(s): _____

Use Finger Cymbals?: _____

Steps to include: _____

_____

Chapter 7

It's Show Time!

This chapter is dedicated to those dancers who are dancing for the very first time. Here are some tips for doing your first show, whether it's an informal Hafla, Dance Recital or first Seminar Show or Restaurant show.

Congratulation! You have gathered enough courage to do your first dance!

Many thoughts run through you mind from remembering the steps to worrying about finger cymbals or any costume issues.

Fear not. Here are some suggestions for those who are belly dancing for the very first time.

START SMALL

The first time dancing does not have to be in front of 100 or even 20 people. As scary as it might sound, the first time performing can be done in front of family members or friends. Trust me, they can be your worst critics, or your most awesome supporters. Sometimes it is easier to dance in front of strangers, rather than family members.

Your family members may think of you as that computer nerd from college or that sci-fi geek who won't miss any episodes of *Star Trek*. Trust me, that describes me. So when it came time to dance for my family, it was very scary.

PRACTICE, PRACTICE, PRACTICE!

So you will feel prepared, prepared, prepared!

I had a dance prepared that I choreographed way back when, *Raks Leyla*. I practiced that dance at least 20 times to make sure I felt comfortable. I had started out buying very inexpensive costumes, that I mixed with a fuller skirt (to hide my legs) so I wouldn't feel overexposed in front of family members.

THE BIG DAY

Surprisingly, went without a hitch because I started small and felt prepared.

I am really big into creating a LIST where I check off everything before any major endeavor. Here is a list for first time dancers that might help your first time go as smoothly.

DANCE PREPARATION FIRST SHOWS

Hafla Show

YOU can organize an informal Hafla (get-together) for yourself or with some of your dance study-buddies. There is strength and support in numbers.

Dance Routine: Feel free to use any of the dance routines in this book, create your own choreography, or find a piece of music you love and dance Free Style! Figure out the exact location where you will be dancing and if you have some private time to practice beforehand in that space, all the better.

Music: Lucky for you, the internet has most of the belly dance MP3 downloads you need. One of my favorite websites to buy belly dance music from is *www.amazon.com*. You can actually preview the music first before you buy it. The cost is very affordable at around $.99 for most single song downloads. Speaking of music, be sure to do a *SOUND CHECK*. Are you planning to use a music CD, cassette tape or MP3 for your performance? Do a sound check with your equipment to make sure the sound is ample enough for the audience. Even more important if you plan to use finger cymbals. There should be enough volume so that you can still hear the music and play the cymbals.

Costumes: Belly Dance costumes are available on the internet through many vendors in various sizes, colors and price ranges. For example, navigate to *www.ebay.com* and you can do a search for many belly dance costumes that are very affordable. Keep in mind the shipping time to make sure the costume arrives well before the Hafla so you can do a "Dress Rehearsal" (practice in your costume) before the Hafla.

Food: Bring the flavor of the middle east to your Hafla or get-together by including Middle Eastern cuisine. Mucho moolah for budget, why have your favorite Greek or Arabic restaurant cater your party. On a budget? Try getting the middle eastern food from your grocery store. Most stores carry the following items:

1. Hummus dip
2. Pita bread
3. Rice Pilaf
4. Ground lamb for Gyros (hamburger patties or bake like a meatloaf)
5. Kebabs (made from chicken, lamb or beef)
6. Feta Cheese
7. Greek Olives (Kalamata)
8. Couscous
9. Baklava (pre-made or buy separate ingredients to make)
10. Greek Salad (enhance a regular salad with feta cheese, greek olives, tomatoes, cucumbers)
11. Taziki Sauce (make your own using cucumbers, lemon juice, greek yogurt, feta, etc.)
12. Dolma (stuffed grape leaves)

I get a lot of my recipes from *www.foodtv.com*, but you can do an internet search for specific recipes on the web.

Dance Recital

If you are part of a dance class, you can participate in a dance recital with your fellow students. I would organize the recitals so that each dance class would perform the dances they had studied the previous month. The recitals would be a mixture of beginner, intermediate, advanced, group and solo performers.

Dance Routine: The beginner students would perform one of the 5 dances from the beginning chapter, the intermediate students would perform one of the intermediate dancers, all dancers could participate in group dances and the more advanced performers would do an advanced dance or solo.

Music: The music was organized by the number to be performed in the show. For example, Act 1 might have 5 performances, Act 2 might have 4 performances and Act 3 might have 3 performances for a total of 10 dances that evening. The tapes or CDs were notated Act 1, #1, Act 3, #2, etc.

Costumes: We used the costumes from my dance troupe, The Scheherazade Dance Company for many of the dancers, some of the dancers had the individual costumes for solo dances and I also loaned out some of my costumes to dancers as well. We would take one hour away from class time to have a costume day to divide the costume colors and make sure the sizes were a good fit.

Seminar Shows

You might be lucky enough to get invited to dance in a seminar show. These shows are a lot of fun because you are dancing in front of your peers and you have an audience that really loves and appreciates dance.

Dance Routine: You want to be extra prepared to dance in front of your peers. So take great care in selecting your music and dance style. It is a good idea to attend the seminar show the year before, or several different seminar shows to get an idea of what the other dancers might be doing. Some shows might be saturated with many dancers doing Egyptian Cabaret style. If you want to fit in then do a similar style, but if you want to stand out, perhaps do a Cane Dance, Sword Dance or something a bit more folkloric. For shows that you dance in again and again every year, you might consider doing something different than what you did the last time. If you did a Cane dance last year, then perhaps this year you will do a Cape dance for example. Sometimes a very popular piece of music comes out that all dancers want to dance to. You have to be very careful in selecting your music so that you don't end up being 3 or 4 dancers, dancing to the same music

Music: Find out which format to provide your music in from the sponsor. Do you need to provide a cassette tape, a CD or can you use MP3 files? Make sure that you clearly label your tape with your name and name of dance. For cassette tapes, you can also include your belly dance business card in the insert so that when the show is over you can easily recognize your tape. When I use CDs for shows, I create a CD label that includes my Dance Name, name of song, date, etc. with a CD case to protect it.

Costumes: I like to show off my new expensive costumes and debut them at a Dance Seminar show, before using them for local performances later on that year. Make sure you wear a Caftan or Cover Up to "hide" your costume before the show, so that it will be a "surprise" when it is time for you to dance.

Restaurant Shows

With enough time and practice a Restaurant or Nightclub owner might ask you to dance in their venue. These are "paid" shows that might require an advance agreement in regards to your pay and any comps (i.e. a free dinner or drinks). With business out of the way, be prepared to dance for the general public.

Dance Routine: These can be choreographed or free style dances performed to pre-taped music or LIVE with the restaurant band. Some restaurants have a very small space to perform, which means that parts of your dance will be performed in a small area, which other parts of the dance can be performed travelling among the audience members to visit while they are eating. Be careful of the audience member needs, if they are busy eating or talking, it might not be a good time to "visit" that particular table. If you have an audience with lots of kids, be sure to include them in your dance performance.

Music: Find out if the restaurant sound system uses a cassette tape or CD. For restaurants that "rotate" different dancers, go and support your fellow dancer by watching her show while making note of the sound volume. Make note of the available dance area. For the most part, you want to perform to the music from the owner's homeland. If the restaurant owner is Egyptian, be sure to use Egyptian music in your dance routines. If you are dancing in a Greek restaurant, feel free to use music that is Greek, Turkish, Armenian, etc. There is no hard, fast rule about this, you can mix and match. But be sure to honor the "theme" of the restaurant, if it is a Greek Cuisine restaurant, you can offer them Greek music in your dance.

Costumes: For restaurant shows, you can show off your flashy, cabaret-style costumes, such as the traditional skirt, veil, bra & belt. If you plan on doing a Turkish/Greek dance, you could incorporate a Turkish Ruffled skirt for your 9/8 Karshlimar part of the dance. If you are doing a Sword dance in the restaurant, you might wear Harem Pants that night. Again, be sure you wear a Caftan or Cover Up to "hide" your costume before the show, so that it will be a "surprise" when it is time for you to dance.

Chapter 8

Dance Gossip & Goodies

About The Author: Shalimar Ali

My dance journey began as a teenager in 1978 when I took my first belly dance class at a local community center. I was shy in class and thought I was one of the worst in my class. I knew I could do the movements, but wasn't very comfortable showing them off. We had a "showoff" in my class and whenever she showed off her moves, I was secretly jealous. I knew I could do the moves, but just didn't have her confidence. Then I told myself, "Hey self, you can do it!" Then I admitted that I really loved Belly Dance and wanted to learn as much as possible, dance and buy the fabulous costumes.

I was so excited after my classes that I would come home and "share" what I learned with my family. I taught my little sister Candy everything that I learned in class. I was too scared to dance for my family for a long time. I did not have a private practice spot in our house, so I would practice in the bathroom with the door locked.

I shopped around and began lessons with 2 other local teachers. I also began teaching classes and choreographing dances to my favorite belly dance songs. My book started out real skinny back in the 1980's and it grew and grew as I added additional choreographies. When I felt I had learned all I could learn locally, I began travelling across the country to take workshops from the best as well as performing in dance seminar shows across the country as well as locally in restaurants. I entered and won some local and national dance competitions.

I have only had one period in my life when I did Belly Dance full-time as a job, back when I briefly danced at an Amusement park one summer. But realistically, I prefer to not have dance as my sole source of income due to lack of job benefits such as health & life insurance, and retirement.

Looking back on my 30+ years in Belly Dance, it was a lot of fun, hard work, sacrifice, sewing, meeting lots of people with the same interest, rehearsing, etc. I'm glad I had the honor or teaching so many students and taking them from "baby" beginners all the way to professional dancers and instructors.

I have had the honor be able to travel to Perform, Learn or Teach dance in the Midwest area (including Missouri, Kansas, Oklahoma, Illinois, Iowa, Nebraska, Wisconsin, Arkansas, Washington, Georgia, New Mexico) as well as New York, California and Montreal, Canada.

And some of my notable career highlights include

- Winning "Miss America of the Belly Dance" in 1989
- Performing at the Dorothy Chandler Pavilion - International Dance Show in 1990
- Dance Workshop Instructor and Performer at the Cairo Carnival in 1993

But the biggest benefit of being involved in Belly Dance is how it personally changed me. I started taking dance lessons at a young age at Smith Sisters Dance Studio and the Caruthers Dance Studio. During high school it was my goal to become a journalist. But, one day I was at my little sister's dance recital in the early 1980s, and a little girl was singing and dancing to "*I Want To Be A Dancer.*" I cried after watching the recital because I knew then that I wanted to be a Belly Dancer. And that was so different from journalism and the career path that I chose in journalism. Well, this caused lots of confusion as I furthered my education in college, knowing I really wanted to dance at that point in my life. So on the weekends, I chose to further my education in dance by attending workshops and seminars, teaching dance classes, watching videos, etc.

This book captures my dance training technique that I used train over 1000 students locally, hope you enjoyed it!

THE SHALIMAR ALI TECHNIQUE & CERTIFICATION PROGRAM

I had the great opportunity to teach over 1000 students and guiding them from Beginner to Advanced student levels, as professional dancers and teachers.

My secret to success was a balance of Dance Technique and Choreography. These students had a choice of dance teachers. They had the option to learn belly dance from any teacher in our community.

Many of them commented that some teachers only taught dance technique, but not how to put a dance together. Further, they said what they liked most about my classes was the opportunity to use the steps learned in an actual dance routine. In other words, they love the fact that they not only learned the dance technique, the steps, turns, etc., but they also saw the technique come together in the form of a dance that they learned.

I divided my classes into Beginning, Intermediate and Advanced Levels. The beginning level dances were easy and basic, because you have to start somewhere. Gradually, as they progressed to each level, they added to their basic movements by learning finger cymbals, veilwork, floorwork, tambourine, cane dance and group dances.

In order to move to the next level, each student had to perform all of the dances in that level. We had a monthly recital so the students could show the dances they learned that month. Once a student had learned and performed all of the Beginner Level dances, they received a Certificate and was allowed to pass to Intermediate Level. Same thing for going from Intermediate Level to Advanced. Then from Advanced to Performer and eventually passing that by creating their own Choreography to pass all levels.

Once they had passed all levels they were prepared to perform in public as well as teach others, which was good for me to have other teacher fill in for classes or if I was unavailable.

I would like to take my *Certification Program* that has been used locally for over 20 years and make it available for any dancer wishing to be certified.

For those students who don't have a local teacher, you are welcome to contact me about private classes at:

http://www.youtube.com/user/Shalimarali

I offer one on one classes at the following website:

http://www.teachstreet.com/teacher/shalimar-ali

You can upload your filmed dance routines so I can view it and mail you the dance certificates:

www.youtube.com

I am also in the process of adding more of the dances to my YouTube channel, so that the students will have a way to follow along with the dances.

Here are some more tips for you to be successful and have fun:

- *Study*

Be serious about studying dance. Go to classes on a regular basis. Take dance workshops in your city and also travel to other city to become exposed to different dancers and dance styles.

- *Perform*

Belly Dance is a Performance Art. The more you do it, the better you'll get. Take every opportunity for a show (family functions, job-related events, belly dance shows, etc.). A dancer who has performed at 20 shows will be a better dancer than a dancer who has performed at 2 shows. Experience is the best teacher.

- *Watch*

Watch other dancers. Watch DVDs of other dancers. Watch belly dancers on TV shows. Watch dancers at restaurant shows. Watch other students in your class. Watch your teacher. Develop and eagle eye. What does one dancer's figure 8 look like compared to another? Are the figure 8's same or different? How are the arms used to frame certain movements? What about facial expressions? Do all dancers use them? Eye contact with the audience. Does the dancer always smile at the audience? Is she only looking dead-ahead? Are other expressions conveyed to the audience like laughter, sensuality, etc.?

- *Track your Studies and Performances*

Write down notes from class sessions. Set goals during rehearsals. Videotape all of your dance performances and watch them. Make a list of 5 new rhythms that you want to learn. Or, write down all of the rhythms that you have learned so far. Write down your choreographies or ideas for free-style dance routines. Keep a notebook for your dance movements, finger cymbal patterns, etc. And keep updating your dance journal.

- *Grow*

Accept new challenges. Maybe you have been studying dance for a few years and suddenly you are invited to fill-in for a sick dancer one weekend at a restaurant. Perhaps this will be your first time dancing at a restaurant and your are scared to death to do it. But, if you never start, how are you going to get better? The sick dancer had a first show at a restaurant long ago. Every dancer has a first time dancing in a bellygram, restaurant show, wedding, etc. Maybe the first time wasn't 100% perfect, but if you try your very best, then that is the best you can expect. Always keep learning. Keep taking workshops, keep taking classes, or start teaching classes or workshops. Never feel that you know everything. Without fresh ideas and new input, even the best of the best can become stale and stunt their dance growth!

The secret to getting the most out of this Dance is to PRACTICE, PRACTICE, PRACTICE and then PRACTICE some more. Every dance instructor can attest to the fact that the student who practices on a regular basis is more likely to be a better dance performer than one who doesn't. So, when you "cheat" on practicing, you only end up "cheating" on yourself as a performer. Learning to Belly Dance is somewhat like putting a jigsaw puzzle together—you need all the pieces that fit together.

Some of the pieces include: Knowing the dance terminology or names of dance movements, knowing how to perform or execute the dance movements learned, knowing how to put the dance movements learned with other dance movements, knowing about the music, culture and rhythms of the middle east so that you'll know how to play them/dance to them, knowing exactly what Belly Dance is and isn't; or having a feel for the music and the art itself. Other things you can de are: attend classes regularly, read all you can on dance, especially Belly Dance, and anything else you can get your hands on about cultures and customs of the middle east; ask questions, especially if you're having problems with a particular dance movement, watch other dancers perform—any and all dance forms, and NEVER, EVER GIVE UP!

What do you hope to get out of belly dancing?

First of all, ask yourself, "Why did I purchase this book?" Then compare your answer with the Book Contents. In a way, this class is what you make out of it if you take it for fun only, then that's probably what you'll get out of it; although the exercise you'll receive along the way certainly won't hurt you. So at the very least you can hope to tone your body through exercise. But at its best, Belly Dance can add a spark to your lift, help you discover your femininity and also—it is a great way to have fun while dancing!

SHALIMAR ALI'S TOP FAVORITE DANCERS

These dancers have taught me, inspired me, motivated me and influenced my dance career.

1. **Sahda Sabri** (Wichita, KS). I met her when she was a judge in the Flamingo Dance Studio Dance Competition in 1981. She invited me to dance at one of her Seminar Shows in Wichita. That was the first seminar show I danced in. I returned to many of her future seminars to study dance or perform. I also travelled there to take private lessons from Sahda. I also sponsored her in a workshop in my town. She provided me the opportunity to study dance with *Mahmoud Reda* (Egypt) the first workshop I attended and later on with *Jodette* (Egypt). Sahda started something big.

2. **Simone** (St. Louis, MO). I used to go to many, many seminar shows in St. Louis to study dance or to perform in the seminar shows. I also travelled there to take private lessons from Simone. She and her dance troupe, Simone's 7th Veils, really took care of me, watched over me and looked after me when I came to St. Louis. To help save money, her dance troupe members would often let me crash there so I wouldn't have to pay for a hotel room. I just love them all. That was my first chance to study with *Suhaila Salimpour* when she was a teenager. A big honor happened once when I was there to take a seminar with Lala Hakim. Her plane was late, so they asked me to fill in briefly until she arrived. What an honor. I just love them all. My best buddy in dance from St. Louis, *Somra*, would also take care of me during my visits. She eventually invited me to teach a workshop in St. Louis, that was a challenge and a lot of fun. And of course I sponsored both Simone and Somra to teach dance workshops in my hometown.

3. **Lala Hakim** (Egypt and Montreal, Canada). I first had a chance to study with Lala Hakim in St. Louis. I loved her style of dance so much that I went to Lala's weekend dance seminar in Montreal, Canada 1983. She was a big influence on my Egyptian Cabaret Dance style. I sponsored Lala in a workshop and I remember her doing 2 dances. First she danced to a recorded song and did a wonderful job. But then she also did an impromptu dance to live music by *Brothers of the Baladi*, who were also here to perform live music for the show. And I really loved the impromptu dance better. It was fabulous!

4. **DeAnn Adams** (Larkspur, CA). Back in the 1980's I flew to her weeklong seminar in California. It was great to see the Dream Dancers in person and hear live music from Light Rain. I sponsored her in

a dance seminar I believe in 1994. She did one thing that no other dance teacher I sponsored did. We had a performance at an ethnic festival, and DeAnn actually came to the performance and cheered us on. I've never forget that. I was so sad to hear that she passed in 2000. She had a powerful influence on dance style, finger cymbals, music, choreography, dance troupe direction and costuming.

5. **Elinor Powell** (Springfield, MA) Love to watch her on Film & TV. Elinor Powell was a kick-butt dancer from the 1930s 1940s, I could see a jazzy, soul influence in her dancing. I love most about her style is her stamina and her turns. Even though she was known for tap, you could also see jazz and acrobats in her dances.

6. **Bob Fosse** (Chicago, IL) Love, love, love *All That Jazz*, one of my all-time favorite movies. His dances staged it all, attitude, costume, hard work and sweat. I wish I could have been there to audition for one of his shows just to have him critique me. His protégée, Ann Reinking, ain't so bad either; love her choreographies in *Bye Bye Birdie*.

Speaking of *Bye Bye Birdie*, a special Shout out to **Vanessa L. Williams** (Millwood, NY)! She is my role model and I love all of her films & TV shows, especially *Soul Food, Dance with Me, Desperate Housewives, Ugly Betty* and *Bye Bye Birdie*. She does a dance in *Bye Bye Birdie* that is burlesque style, sort of similar to Belly Dance—love it. I'll never forget the day that she stepped down from her *Miss America* title. I believed that she was set up and that the pageant knew about the photos before she was crowned. But she stepped down with such grace and dignity, it was a real inspiration for me to enter the *Miss America of the Belly Dance* pageant because I wanted to be like her. I entered the pageant twice, first in 1988 and again in 1989. I did a terrible job dancing the first time because I was so nervous I dropped my cymbals. I felt bad the entire year and vowed that I would go back just to prove to myself that I can dance without dropping my cymbals (rookie mistake). I was surprised to win the next year in 1989. She was born in the same year as my sister Gina, so when I watch her, I sort of pretend that I can see how Gina would look if she were still alive. Thanks for the inspiration Vanessa.

7. **Debbie Allen** (Houston, TX) The triple threat who can sing, act and dance! I saw a special on Debbie Allen and she did a Belly Dance in a yellow costume. Caught ya Belly Dancing! But I love all of her choreographies, in particular the opening for the Cosby Show and the 1993 Oscar Awards for A Whole New World featuring Atlantis, Veena & Neena

8. **Morocco** (New York, NY) The very first time I rode in an airplane was to fly to New York back in 1981 to attend a weeklong seminar

with Morocco (Aunt Rocky). I soaked up all of the ethnic flavors that were taught that week and was introduced to styles like Guedra, Sudanese and Dervish dance. I was very lucky to be able to attend that seminar and future seminars with Morocco, because she is the dance teacher and performer of our lifetime, a *Legend*! I sponsored her in a seminar in my local area and it was an honor to have her here. She has a book coming out soon that will be fabulous! I can't wait for it, so be sure to check it out.

9. ***Josephine Baker*** (St. Louis, MO) What a Diva! Love her hair, makeup and costumes, well the ones that covered the boobs. Never met her, never studied with her, never saw her in person before she died in 1975. But, when I was a kid I remember seeing her photos in *Jet* magazine. I was drawn to her costumes, makeup and hair styles. Tried my best to imitate her hair. When I first read about how she went to Paris and became a sensation, I could not believe that a black woman could do that, especially back in the 1920s. Her dance style was very different from Middle Eastern Belly Dance, in that we don't dance topless (all kidding about the 1960 belly dance pasties aside). Not something I would ever do, as my entire family has to be able to watch me dance, including the kids, my mom & dad, and my pastor uncle. But she was a very powerful performer and civil rights activist. I dare say she is a role model that I never got to meet.

As Close to Perfection

There are many top dancers in the world from the famous Egyptian Dancers Nagwa Fouad and Sohair Zaki as well as famous American dancers like Bert Balladine, Serena and Jamila Salimpour. As close to perfection in belly dance is **Suhaila Salimpour**. Her family has 3 generations of dance, mom Jamila, daughter Suhaila and granddaughter Isabella. I remember studying with Suhaila when she was a teenager teaching a dance workshop in St. Louis, MO. She had such power and control over ladies who were twice her age in the workshop. Her choreographies are legendary. I still have some of her dance videos from the 1980s as well as her recent DVDs. My granddaughters love watching Isabella dance. They imitate her on the DVD. The proof is in the pudding, just watch Suhaila dance, look at the dancers she has taught who pass down her technique and also watch her dance troupe perform on DVD. PERFECTION!

Shalimar Ali's Top Favorite Students

My students were amazing! They inspired me to create choreographies and personalize the dances to fit them as needed. It was an honor to teach Bonnie, Julie, Cathy, Judy, Joyce, Ellen, Sharon, Angela and all the rest.

SHALIMAR ALI'S FAVORITE DANCE DVDs/VIDEOs

Dance DVDs & Videos are a great way to exercise and learn new dance technique. I love buying new dance videos to get fresh ideas for dances, movements and costumes. Here are 3 of my favorites:

1. ***World Dance New York*** Love, love love their instructional and performance DVDs! Neon is absolutely fabulous, as well as all of the dancers in their DVDs with a special shout out to Azmara for all of the emotion she portrays in her dancing. My love the *Love Potion* DVD workout and watching the performances in the Fantasy Bellydance DVD. These ladies took belly dance to a whole new level in regards to theatrics, staging, emotion and production values. They have a wide variety of belly dance DVDs available for instruction or to watch performances, which I highly recommend.

2. ***Veena & Neena*** I am a huge fan and I have most of their Belly Dance DVDs as well as their book, *The Way of the Belly*. In addition to their belly dance DVDs you can catch them performing on many TV shows, such as Steve Harvey, One on One, etc. My favorite exercise DVD is Slim Down, that which gives a good workout. But each and every one of their DVDs are highly recommended.

3. ***Rania*** This lady really gives a good workout in her DVDs, and Rania, I still have a hard time keeping up with you, but I will keep trying, LOL. I love the beautiful performances at the end of the videos as well. Highly recommended.

SHALIMAR ALI'S FAVORITE DANCE COSTUMERS

Doyne Allen (Long Beach, CA). He created my top 5 favorite costumes. The multi-color jeweled costume I'm wearing in the cover photo. Also he did my pharonic costume that has a bra, belt and attached skirt that is completely beaded. It weighs about 20 pounds and I always lose weight whenever I dance in it. He made a copper & gold beaded bra & belt that has light a Tiger tail that I wear with leopard print skirts. He also made a Silver & Multi-color Bra & Belt that has large hologram paillettes. And I have to mention the fabulous Red and Gold bra & belt he did.

Nazaree (Chicago, IL). I consider her a friend and sister dancer. She has made many beautiful crocheted sequin Dazzler hip scarves, vests and sequin skirts. I remember her as being the originator of the Dazzler hip scarves. She sponsored me to teach a few workshops in Chicago and she is an extremely talented designer and fabulous dancer.

Julia & Mesmera (California). If you have seen Julia's costumes, they are all very beautiful. She created an Orange, Silver and Pearl costume for me that I really love. I remember seeing Mesmera belly dance on TV shows like *Mama's Family*. I actually sponsored both Julia and Mesmera to teach a dance seminar in my hometown. The belly dance world can sometimes be a very cutthroat, cat fight environment. But I remember that Julia and Mesmera were above the cat fighting and would actually encourage and help other dancers. I asked Mesmera who created the Cape that she used in one of her dance videos and she actually told me. I had one copied that was just like hers. Not many dancers would share their information.

Audrena (Chicago, IL) first saw her at Sahda Sabri's Dance Convention back in the early 1980s that featured Mahmood Reda. Love ordering costumes from Audrena. She really takes care of her customers and her costumes are gorgeous!

Yasmeen Samra (Palo Alto, CA) I remember her magazine, The Belly Dancer Magazine and she also sold costumes. One of the very first places I purchased costuming accessories via mail order back in 1979. I saw her perform in person in Fort Worth, TX at a show that featured Bert Balladine and George Abdo. Also the first time I met Amaya. Yasmeen really advanced Belly Dance with her magazine and costuming and was a personal role model for me as well.

SHALIMAR ALI'S FAVORITE MUSICIANS

1. **Raja Zahr**: I love his music, the beat, the way it is created for dancers. I sponsored Raja & John Bilezikjian to perform live music at one of our seminar shows. They were just as fabulous as their music tapes and CDs. I first met Raja in person at the Cairo Carnival in 1983. I had choreographed a dance to *Rugisnee* and I asked him what it meant, and he said *make me dance slowly*. I have danced to many shows using Raja's music and in particular love his drum solos.

2. **Brothers of the Baladi**: This is an Old School band from the 1980s that keeps on ticking. I have choreographed many of their songs and some favorites include *Tamzara*. I sponsored them to perform live music at one of our seminar shows and I remember Michael Beach getting really involved with the dancers onstage. He was up drumming with me when I was doing my drum solo. I'll never forget that. Michael is also someone who shares. I wrote a letter to them

back in the 1980s to find out what font they used on their belly dance cassette tape *Dance with Gladness*. He wrote me back and told me which font it was.

3. **Eddie Kochak**: Never met him or saw him perform in person. But back when I first started learning belly dance, Eddie Kochak Volume 1 - 5 was the bomb! I still have all of them on LP. *Note*: back in the old days, we had belly dance music on LPs and we would transfer them to cassette for shows. But I still remember taking classes where LPs were used. I have lots of choreographies to many of his albums, some favorites include: *Connie Sudanese*, *Phaedra Pharonica*, *Dance Ramza* and *Hanna Drumzilzia*. I loved the LP artwork cover that showed Ibrahim Farrah and many of his top dancers. The costumes were inspiring. I would like to think that Eddie Kochak's Amer-Arabic sound was responsible for helping Americans digest Middle Eastern music. This **Cross-Over** made Belly Dance music *easy on the ears* for the audience and dancer.

SEARCHING FOR THE MUSIC USED IN THIS BOOK

Some of the music used for the choreographies date back to the early 1980's so you may be wondering how you are going to find music from 30 years ago.

Back in the late 1970s and early 1980s most of the music was on vinyl LP albums. From the 1980s to 1990s cassette tape music was popular. Then from the 1990s to 2000s belly dance music came in CD form.

So here are some ways to search for the songs used for the dances where I have listed the name of the Artist, Album and Song:

1. **Internet Search**: Use Google and other search engines to type in the artist name and song title. You may get hits for the song in MP3 format at Amazon or Itunes. Sometimes the search will pull up a website created by the musician (i.e. The Brothers of the Baladi, Hossam Ramzy, Raja Zahr, etc.). If you pull up a website that has the song available for download, you can also listen to a clip first before buying

2. **Maqam Music**: You can find a lot of the songs used at *www.maqam. com*.

3. **BHUZ**: All things Belly Dance. You can post a note to other dancers who may have a copy of the music to help you find it at *www.bhuz.com*.

4. **Local Libraries** I was surprised to find so many belly dance CDs at my library. I did a search online using the library database search and was able to find George Abdo and Eddie Kochak. Also the library is

a great place to check out belly dance videos and DVDs to use and try them before you buy them.

5. **YouTube**: If you really, really get stuck searching for the music used in this book and can't find it, please view the videos that will be released at: *http://www.youtube.com/user/Shalimarali*

You can actually play the videos and dance along to the music.

BELLY DANCE TEST ANSWER KEY

For Teachers Only (students please don't peak)

NOTE: The answers do not need to match exactly. For example, one question might ask to name 2 floor movements, any floor movement could be used as a possible answer. So if the answers don't exactly match what is printed here, please pass the answer if it actually answers the questions. No wrong score should be given if it answers the question, but does not exactly match my answers.

BEGINNER DANCE EXAMINATION & CHECKLIST

The student needs a passing score of 80% or more (4 out of 5 questions)

Student Name: _____

Instructor Name: _____

Exam Date _____

1. In what countries did Middle Eastern Dance originate?
   a. Egypt
   b. Turkey
   c. Africa
   d. Greece
   e. Lebanon, and many other countries would be acceptable

2. Define the term *"Belly Dance"* **Belly dance** or Bellydance is a "Western"-coined name for a traditional *"Middle Eastern"* dance, especially **raqs sharqi** (*Arabic*: يقرش صقر). It is sometimes also called **Middle Eastern dance** or **Arabic dance** in the West, or by the *Greco-Turkish* term **çiftetelli** (*Greek*: τσιφτετέλι), though in the Middle East it is often called **Oriental dance.**

- **Raqs sharqi** (*Arabic*: يقرش صقر; literally "oriental dance") is the style more familiar to Westerners, performed in restaurants and *cabarets* around the world. It is more commonly performed by female dancers but is also sometimes danced by men. It is a *solo improvisational* dance, although students often perform *choreographed* dances in a group.
- **Raqs baladi**, (*Arabic*: يدلب صقر; literally "dance of country", or *"folk"* dance) is the folkloric style, danced socially by men and

women of all ages in some Middle Eastern countries, usually at festive occasions such as weddings. [*Source*: Wikipedia]

3. What four basic body parts can be isolated?
    a. Head or neck
    b. Rib Cage
    c. Shoulders
    d. Hips

4. Name and illustrate six directions that most body parts can move or be isolated in:
    a. right
    b. left
    c. front
    d. back
    e. up
    f. down

5. What can be four basic components/parts of veil dancing:
    a. Draping (pre-show)
    b. Undraping
    c. Veil dancing (poses, flutter, turns, swirls, matador, etc.)
    d. Discarding

Dance Performance Checklist, the student must perform the following dances before advancing to the Intermediate Level:

Beginning Level

_____ Raks Leyla, cabaret with finger cymbals to 4/4
_____ Jasmine Dancer, cabaret w/veil and finger cymbals
_____ Varter, veil dance
_____ Bedouin Wedding, cane dance to beledi
_____ Tomzara, tambourine dance to 9/8

INTERMEDIATE DANCE EXAMINATION & CHECKLIST

The student needs a passing score of 80% or more (4 out of 5 questions)

Student Name: _____

Instructor Name: _____

Exam Date: _____

1. What are step variations: Any modifications or alterations of a basic step, for example: Hip Circle in a Circle, Basic Karshlimar with a Hop, Figure 8 with a Bounce, etc. (Usually, the variant is not a step in itself.)

    Give an example: You can add a bounce to a hip circle, say you are using 8 counts, then bounce the heels each time for a total of 8 bounces added to the hip circle, making it Hip Circle with a bounce.

2. What are step combinations: Joining similar or different steps together, for example: Camel Walk with Rib Circle, Basic Karshlimar with a Hip Shimmy, etc. (Usually the combined step is a step that can be performed by itself.)

    Give an example: You can combine 2 or 3 like a Shoulder Shimmy, plus Undulation, plus Rib Drop

3. What are step transitions: Take you from one step into a different step, gracefully, for example: going from Hip Circle into a Walking Hip Shimmy smoothly (movements aren't "choppy" or "jerky")

4. Name 3 different ways to play finger cymbals:
    a. Clack
    b. Click
    c. Trill
    d. Mute

5. Name 2 other words for finger cymbals:
    a. Zills
    b. Sagat

Dance Performance Checklist, the student must perform the following dances before advancing to the Advanced Level:

Intermediate Level

> _____ Ambera, cabaret w/cape entrance
> _____ Tamzara, group tambourine dance to 9/8
> _____ Amayaguena/El Porompompero
> _____ The Sword Dance
> _____ Kalamatiano, skirt dance to 7/8

ADVANCED DANCE EXAMINATION & CHECKLIST

The student needs a passing score of 80% or more (4 out of 5 questions)

Student Name: _____

Instructor Name: _____

Exam Date: _____

1. Name 3 types of Rib Movements:
   a.   Rib lift or drop
   b.   Rib thrust or slide
   c.   Rib circle or figure 8

2. Name 6 types of hip movements that have the word "hip" in it
   a.   Hip circle
   b.   Hip shimmy up & down
   c.   Hip thrust
   d.   Hip shimmy twisting
   e.   Hip lift or drop
   f.   Hip figure 8, maya or hip camel

3. Name 2 variations for hip figure 8:
   a.   Hip figure 8 with a bounce
   b.   Hip figure 8 with 1 heel up

4. Name 3 travel directions for hip drops or lifts:
   a.   Diagonal to right or left
   b.   To right or left side
   c.   In circle to right or left

5. Name two floor dance movements:
   a.   Hip circle in a circle
   b.   Floor turn, or many other answers would pass

Dance Performance Checklist, the student must perform the following dances before advancing to the Group/Troupe Level:

Advanced Level

_____   Bahia
_____   Zannube, 4-Part Cabaret
_____   Welcome to the Dance, YaSalaam
_____   Uskudar, Turkish cabaret w/finger cymbals
_____   Ro-He cape entrance, Baladi Thriller

GROUP/TROUP DANCE EXAMINATION & CHECKLIST

The student needs a passing score of 80% or more (4 out of 5 questions)

Student Name: _____

Instructor Name: _____

Exam Date: _____

1. When dancing in group formation with 4 dancers, describe 2 different formations to arrange the group in:
    a. The group can be arranged in 4 points using the front right, front left, back right and back left areas of the stage in a square pattern.
    b. You can also arrange a diamond pattern by having a dancer in center front, center back, middle right and middle left areas of the stage.

2. Can all solo dances be adapted to use for a group or troupe dance?
    a. Yes _X_
    b. No
    c. If no, then why There could be many possible reasons why you should not adapt some solo dances to group dances, ranging from available stage space (could be large enough for a solo dancer, but not have enough space for 3 or 4 dancers); to the purpose/intent of the dance, say a soloist is hired for a nightclub show and they only want 1 dancer, you are choreographing the dance specifically for a soloist, rather than a group. While that is true, many if not most of the dances created for a soloist can be adapted as a group dance.

3. Besides a group cane dance, name 6 other props that a dance troupe can use when performing a group dance:
    a. Sword
    b. Tambourine
    c. Candles
    d. Basket
    e. Fans
    f. Veils or Capes

4. Is it a rule that all dance group members should perform the same exact steps at the same exact time in a group choreography?
    a. Yes _____
    b.   No _x_
    c.   If yes, then why While it is easier to choreograph all group members performing the exact same step at the exact same time, there is no rule that says you have to. You can certainly have 1 dancer doing a spotlight dance in a veil dance while the other dancers are in the background. Or you can have 2 members of a sword dance doing a sword "click" while the others are doing something else.

5. Name 2 of your favorite American Belly Dance Troupes and at least 1 International Belly Dance Troupe: List your own favorites here, any answer could be correct
    a.   World Dance New York
    b.   DeAnn's Dream Dancers
    c.   Ibrahim Farrah Near East Dance Group

Dance Performance Checklist, the student must perform the following dances before advancing to the Performer Level:

Group Level

    _____ Hanna Drumzilzia, drum solo w/finger cymbals
    _____ A Whole New World, group veil dance
    _____ Phaedra Pharonica, pharonic candle dance
    _____ I Remember Egypt, sword dance
    _____ Yahlewa, Canes, Tambourine & Zills

PERFORMER DANCE EXAMINATION & CHECKLIST

The student needs a passing score of 80% or more (8 out of 10 questions)

Student Name: _____

Instructor Name: _____

Exam Date: _____

1. Name five (5) different Belly Dance styles:
    a. Spanish fusion
    b. Egyptian Cabaret
    c. Greek Cabaret
    d. Folkloric, i.e. Cane Dance
    e. Goth

2. What is Choreography? the art of creating and arranging dances-basically. When done well, the result will be a seemingly effortless, inspiring performance combining good use of space, skill, positioning, and uniformity of movement
    What is Free Style? Winging it, or performing steps and/or finger cymbals, veils, etc. to a known rhythm or song without the benefit of knowing what steps or combinations to do beforehand.

3. Name five rhythm accompaniments, identify which 2 are "natural":
    a. Finger Snapping, natural
    b. Hand Clapping, natural
    c. Finger Cymbals
    d. Tambourines
    e. Castanets, tapping the cane while dancing, anything else that adds "sound"

4. Name 5 of your favorite Belly Dance DVDs or Videos, some you already own or search the internet for this answer. Your answers do not need to match mine, just list your favorites:
    a. Veena & Neena, Slim Down
    b. World Dance New York, Love Potion
    c. Belly Dance Superstars Live at the Follies Bergere
    d. Suhaila Salimpour, Bellydance Performance Ensemble with Suhaila
    e. Rania, Advanced Choreography: Modern Egyptian

5. Name three nationally known Middle Eastern musicians who have recorded albums or tapes, include the name of their album or tape for extra credit. You can name anyone in this list, your answer does not have to match mine:
   a. Adam Basma, *Arabic Dance Ensemble, Mobi, Bellydance with Basma,* etc.
   b. Dr. Samy Faraq, *Jewel of the Desert, Arabian Melodies, Balady Fantasy,* etc.
   c. Hossam Ramzy, *Ro-He, Solo Tabla I, II & III, Egyptian Rai,* etc.

6. Name five "specialty dances" that involve the use of "Props":
   a. Basket
   b. Snake
   c. Cane
   d. Sword
   e. Tambourine

7. Balance techniques (name 5 places a cane or sword can be balanced on:
   a. Head
   b. Hip
   c. Shoulder
   d. Chest
   e. Knee

8. What can cane dancing consist of:
   a. Steps
   b. Twirls
   c. Balance

9. A "Cabaret Dance" can consist of six different parts, name and describe them:
   a. Entrance dance
   b. Veil Dance
   c. Stage Dance
   d. Floor Work or Taxim
   e. Drum Solo
   f. Finale

10. Give a finger cymbal pattern that can be used with the following rhythms:
    a. 4/4 RLRLRLRL
    b. 9/8 R L R, LRL
    c. beledi R, LR, LR; L-R-L

Dance Performance Checklist, the student must perform the following dances before completing all levels:

Performer Level

- _____ Dance Ramza/Selma/Nazira,
- _____ Sahara City
- _____ Badia
- _____ Faqset el Fadaa, Veil, stage dance, finale
- _____ Rugisnee, cape dance, Yani drum solo
- _____ Assignment: Choreograph a 5-Part Dance Routine that is 8-10 Minutes Long

DANCE CERTIFICATION FAQ

Common questions about this certification program

1. What is the cost for the certification program?

   The certification program is free to participate in. When each level is completed, I will email the certificate to you. If you would like to have them mailed to an address, there is a $5.00 administrative charge to mail them.

2. Do I have to do the certification program, or can I just take the classes for fun or exercise?

   Yes, you certainly can. There is no obligation to do the certification program, it is only for those dancers who desire certification. Feel free to use the information in this book for knowledge, fun, exercise and happy, carefree dancing.

3. Is it possible to have additional training for either the book content or for the certification program?

   Yes, that is possible as I offer classes through TeachStreet: http://www.teachstreet.com/teacher/shalimar-ali

4. What do the certificates look like?

   Rather than printing a blank template in this book, I would prefer to email the templates to the instructor so they can certify you or email the actual signed certificate directly. But here is a sample of what the certificate can look like:

Certificate of Achievement

Completed the "Students 101" Dance Techniques

Student Name

Beginning Belly Dance Level

Made in the USA
Lexington, KY
19 April 2013